BANQUET MANAGEMENT AND ROOM DIVISION

DR. D.K. Aggarwal
PRINCIPAL
INSTITUTE OF HOTEL MANAGEMENT &
CATERING TECHNOLOGY
BHOPAL (M.P.)

AMAN PUBLICATIONS
NEW DELHI (INDIA)

Published by
Rajiv Jain for Aman Publications
LG-4A, Ganpati Bhawan,
4675-B/21, Ansari Road,
Darya Ganj, Delhi - 110002
PH: 23255012, 23282127
E-mail: sshjbs@yahoo.com

First Edition 2006
ISBN-81-8204-026-4 (HB)

SOLE DISTRIBUTOR
JINDAL BOOK SERVICES
LG-4A, Ganpati Bhawan,
4675-B/21, Ansari Road,
Darya Ganj, Delhi - 110002

Laser Typesetting by:
S.M. Graphics, Delhi,

Printed by:
NCT Printers & Publishers , Delhi, India

Preface

The book *Banquet Management and Room Division* is designed for use by all food service serving staff members. It covers every aspect of banquet service for the positions of host, waiter or waitress, head waiter, banquet manager and other food service staff. It emphasises the service aspects that will distinguish an outstanding guest experience and a successful food service operation. It spells out the rules and techniques of banquet management, room division, event organisation, waiter service, table manners and guest entertaining.

For persons who are responsible for the efficient and profitable operation of a dining room or banquet facility, this book will be a handy reference and training resource, which help them to meet their goals. For service training programmes in organisations providing banquet and/or dining room services, this book will be a thorough and clearly presented guide on the finer points of outstanding service, the distinguishing factor toward creating and maintaining a profitable business. The manager who trains his or her staff using this book and the techniques presented here will provide excellent service to their guests. Students will learn confidence and skills that will serve them well as they serve your guests professionally and efficiently.

CONTENTS

1

Banquet Service

A banquet is a large public meal or feast, complete with main courses and desserts. It usually serves a purpose, such as a charitable gathering, a ceremony, or a celebration. Sometimes a banquet consists of only desserts. To banquet means to treat to a feast or to partake in a feast.

Role of Banquet Managers

Banquet managers plan, organise and direct the service of food and beverages for banquets and other social functions. Duties and responsibilities vary from one position to another but, in general, banquet managers:

— discuss requirements with customers and take detailed notes about banquet requirements

— develop banquet menus in consultation with caterers, chefs or cooks

— prepare budgets

— determine requirements for serving staff and supplies

— supervise everything from the set up prior to the function to the clean up afterward

— develop work schedules and supervise food services during the function

— maintain proper liquor controls and monitor alcohol service
— ensure that equipment is properly cleaned and maintained
— follow up with clients after functions and deal with customer complaints
— hire, train and supervise staff to ensure that service standards are met.

In smaller organisations, banquet managers may assist staff with functions such as setting up the room. In larger organisations, the duties listed above may be divided among several managers and supervisors. For example, where banquet managers and catering managers have separate roles, catering managers discuss banquet requirements with customers and work with chefs and food and beverage managers to develop menus.

Banquet managers often work long hours that include evenings, weekends and holidays. Assisting staff may sometimes involve heavy lifting.

Banquet managers need the following characteristics:
— good communication, supervisory and problem-solving skills
— excellent organisational skills
— the ability to pay close attention to details
— the ability to work alone or as part of a team
— the ability to remain calm while working in close quarters with others during busy periods
— flexibility and creativity.

They should enjoy:
— co-ordinating information and the activities of others
— setting work schedules, monitoring staff and controlling inventory

— negotiating arrangements with suppliers and clients.

Educational Qualifications

There are no standard minimum education requirements for banquet managers but related education is becoming increasingly important. Most employers require banquet managers to have food and beverage service training, food safety training and experience in dining room management. Food allergy training is an asset.

Banquet managers are employed by hotels and hospitality centres such as convention centres. Advancement opportunities vary depending on the banquet manager's qualifications and the size and nature of the employing organisation.

Role of Assistant Banquets Manager

Responsible for the proper application, demonstration, inventory and A/V setup in accordance with company policies

Provide positive contributions to the growth, profitability and image of the company by overseeing and directing standards of excellence within the banquet service staff, banquet set-up staff and audio/visual staff.

Sales

- The position is responsible for initiating and maintaining high quality service efforts that will increase the number of catering functions from both new and previous clients.
- Handling the planning and execution of service for all functions involving banquet food, beverage and meeting services.

— Drive overall topline sales through upsale of food and wine menu items.

— Demonstrate audio/visual capabilities to prospective clients to maximise revenue potential.

Service

— Assume service duties of Banquet Manager in his/her absence.

— Set up and execution of all audio/visual details as they pertain to meeting rooms

— Attend all pre-conference meetings.

— Call clients and internal customers to confirm audio/visual needs.

— Prepare computer and video projection systems for clients in terms of downloading materials/programs.

— Set up complex sound systems program meeting room lighting.

— Offer advanced technical support for guests in the area of lighting and sound while meeting is in progress.

— Install telephones in guest rooms and meeting rooms where necessary coordinate high-sped Internet access between hotel and outside vendor.

Supervision

— Assume supervisory duties of Banquet Manager in his/her absence.

— Coordinate activities of banquet set-up and audio/visual staff.

— Supervise the inventories of audio/visual equipment

— Ensure all banquet staff observe safety guidelines while at work.

— Assist Banquet Manager in administrative responsibilities of banquets, including payroll, tip disbursement, communications, budgeting and client relations.

Inventory Maintenance

— Maintain quality of physical items: tables, chairs, equipment, linen, uniforms.

— Place necessary purchase orders for the replacement of existing operating equipment and the acquisition of new products and services

— Maintain the appearance of the banquet rooms and foyers: wood work, carpeting, lighting, etc.

— Maintain audio/visual equipment and its components.

Human Resources

— Approve the hiring, discipline, evaluation, and terminating of all positions under direct supervision.

— Ensure all associates attend orientations.

— Complete performance reviews with employees as scheduled.

— Ensure fair and equitable treatment of all Banquet staff as well as other support staff.

— Ensure corporate policies and procedures are followed.

Training

— Set and maintain service standards for all position including grooming codes.

— Maintain and update all training certification materials on a timely basis.

— Maintain an on-going training program for all newly hired staff.

— Cross train associates in audio/visual and set-up positions.
— Provide instruction and on-going training of computer hardware and software as it relates to the audio/visual department.
— Conduct daily shift meetings.
— Ensure all set-up and audio/visual employees are aware of policies.
— Drive continuous safety education.

Financial

— Monitor and control labor costs.
— Monitor and control workmens compensation as it impacts the banquet department.
— Monitor and control operating expenses.
— Plan and update monthly and yearly financial plans.
— Responsible for the integrity of the tip distribution process.

Banquet Catering

Food is definitely the star in the catering world, but it's only one part of the equation. As catering companies have moved toward the full-service, event-planning model, the focus has morphed. It's not that food is no longer a focal point, but rather that it is part of a broader mission. Catering is about satisfying all the senses:

— Sight
— Hearing
— Touch
— Smell
— Taste

Today caterers want every aspect of an event to be just as perfect as the food. With the right atmosphere, you can appeal to all of these senses in a way that makes an event special and memorable. Of course, beautifully prepared food can appeal to your sense of taste, smell and sight - perhaps even touch, but it shouldn't outshine the rest of the event. Caterers today generally want every piece of the puzzle, from the decor to the glassware, to have that same kind of impact.

From flatware to flowers, lighting to linens and tables to tunes, everything should complement the food to create a unified overall experience. According to Dondis, continuity is key. You want every aspect to be in sync with each other. For example:

— Does the venue fit the occasion, climate and group size? No matter how lovely the surrounding gardens, you probably wouldn't want to have formally attired guests dining outside in 98-degree weather.

— Does the menu fit the occasion and tastes of the group? For a retirement celebration, where the retiree is getting ready to embark on a 6-month sabbatical in Spain with her spouse, tappas stations would be an inspired idea.

— Does the decor suit the venue and event? White linen, china and crystal stemware might not be the most appropriate table setting for a casual, pool-side barbecue reception. Festive prints, such as blue and white checked tablecloths and matching napkins with plain glass plates and mason jars might be a better fit.

After you make contact with a catering firm, the caterer's first job is to figure out what you want and decide how their company can create it for you. This process usually begins with a client-caterer meeting—sort of like a first date. Whether it happens during the initial phone call or a scheduled appointment, the client services representative wants to get as much information as they can to help them prepare a proposal for you. As a client, you should be ready to answer these questions:

— What is the proposed date and time of the event?

— Is this a social or professional function?

— Do you have a general budget in mind?

— How many guests will attend?

— Have you selected a venue or setting?

Of course, depending on the type of function, other questions can (and should) come into conversation. Keep in mind that this initial discussion is critical because it will be the backbone of the caterer's proposal. So, if you have certain ideas in mind, you need to be as explicit as possible.

The catering company can work with the florist to create centerpieces to match the table setting. One of the biggest mistakes a client can make is to only think about the budget. You can't expect to say to a caterer "I have "x" amount to spend; what can I get for that?" and get a reasonable answer. You also need to explain what you hope to get for that budget. When the caterer understands your budget and your expectations, he or she can figure out if they match-up. If they do, great. If they don't, then don't worry—it's not a wash. It just means that it's time for more questions. Remember you're dealing with professionals and they're equipped to help you.

Let's say you're planning a 50th wedding anniversary for your parents, and like most of us, you're on a pretty strict budget. Initially you have something really elaborate in mind. But, you discover that with the number of guests you hope to invite, your budget isn't going to afford you the luxurious event you envisioned. So it's time to prioritise. The client services representative asks you a series of questions related to your parent's tastes—perhaps something like this:

— What is their favorite kind of food?

— Do they like formal or informal functions?

— When they entertain, what are their gatherings like?

— Do they prefer small or large groups?

— What do your parents like to do in their spare time?

— What's their favorite vacation destination?

From your answers, it's clear that your parents would be much more comfortable with a relaxed, casual atmosphere.

Instead of a formal seated dinner with assigned seating and place-cards, your parents would much rather everyone be able to move about and socialise. A new vision starts to take shape in your mind: An outdoor southern-inspired cocktail party with fairy lights in the trees, soft jazz playing in the background and a light scent of magnolia blossoms swirling around the guests. With this new information, the catering firm can prepare a proposal that accommodates both your expectations and your budget.

The Proposal

The foundation of a proposal is the information gathered during an initial inquiry or meeting with the prospective client:

— type of event

— date

— time

— guest count

— venue

— favourite foods or menu ideas

Armed with these guidelines, the caterer can build a detailed proposal that includes the actual menu, beverages, an itemised listing for equipment rental, the staff requirements and any necessary food or beverage taxes. When planning a proposal, caterers generally consider several other factors in addition to the basic information. The time of day and length of an event can also dictate how much food you need. A party held right after work, during "cocktail hour", say from 5:00 to 7:00 p.m. could center around hors d'oeuvres and other light fare because the guests will probably have plans for dinner after the reception.

Other menu planning considerations include:

— *Balanced menu*—a standard menu should include a balance of two proteins (meat, poultry or seafood), one vegetable and one starch (pasta, rice or potatoes).

— *Courses*—for seated dinners with multiple courses, each course should complement the next and there should be some variety. For example, if you're having a beef entree, then you might consider a seafood appetizer.

— *Buffets*—the number of buffet stations corresponds to the number of guests. If the guest list is large, say 750 or more, you can increase the number of guests per buffet ratio to one buffet per 100 guests.

When the proposal is ready, the caterer gives it to the client for his or her perusal. After the client accepts the proposal, the caterer schedules another meeting to discuss the decor and layout and to plan a detailed timeline of the event.

Making Plans

Caterers and other event planners today have many useful tools to assist them in planning the perfect event. One product, called Room Viewer, automates the process of drawing up floor plans for events and parties. Whether indoors or out, no matter the shape or specs of the room, this computer aided design (CAD) software helps the caterer utilise the space to its best potential.

Caterers can make print-outs showing exactly where everything should go (even down to the placement of utensils) so the catering staff will have a precise map of the event. These print-outs are especially helpful when caterers work with outside vendors, such as equipment rental companies that supply everything from tables and chairs to linen and china.

In addition to CAD-based software programs, there are many business-management software packages specially suited for catering and the food-service industry.

Using a caterer for a dinner party at your home gives you more time to spend with your guests. Two software packages that are particularly useful for catering businesses are "Visual Synergy Small Business" and "Visual Synergy Enterprise." Some of the handy features of these products are:

Visual synergy small business

— Full Sales & Revenue Management Tool
— Event Calendar Management and Event Schedule Reports
— Customer Marketing - Tracking and Reporting
— Revenue Management for Food, Beverage, Equipment, Staff & Miscellaneous items
— Packing Lists for Production and Warehousing
— Event Staff Scheduling and Reporting
— Proposal/Contracts & Invoicing

Visual synergy enterprise

— Proposal & Contract Creations
— Sales Prospects & Contract Management
— Recipe Costing & Purchase Orders
— Inventory Tracking & Reservation Priorities
— Custom Report Writer
— Track Event Profitability
— Event Labor Scheduling & Management

Detailed Schedule

One of the most valuable tools in planning and executing an event is a detailed schedule. Depending on the nature and length of an event, these itineraries can be several pages long, covering each moment, from setup to service to breakdown almost minute-by-minute. Large events may have 100 or more staff members on hand. These schedules are a script of exactly what should happen and when; providing direction to each of the many staff involved.

Caterers have to consider several factors before finalising the schedule. Set-up time is a big consideration. For example, if an event is outside, with no set structures, the caterer might need a couple of days to get the site ready, depending on the number of tents, decor and layout. Cleanup is also a major concern.

The caterer also needs to consider the nature of the gathering. If it's a wedding reception being held in a different location from the ceremony, will all the guests arrive on time? If there is a cocktail reception, how long should that last prior to the dinner? The caterer also has to leave time for a bouquet toss, toasts and the cake cutting. If the event is at a rented facility with a strict end-time, the team has to precisely time and execute all this according to the schedule.

Keep in mind that some facilities do book more than one event in a day. If you're arranging a morning function and have the place booked until 3:00 p.m., that means you, all of your guests, the catering crew, and all their equipment and supplies must be off-premise by 3:00 p.m. sharp.

Prep-Time

In addition to planning the schedule, there's other preliminary work that needs to be done. Before the event, the catering firm's Kitchen Administrator examines the menu and decides what to order. Visual Synergy Software may play a big role in this part of the job. The kitchen staff enters precise measurements to create a detailed database of recipes. The staff can easily expand these recipes to suit any number of guests. Once the team has the right recipe for the appropriate group size, it's easy to see what they need to order.

For a corporate event for 300 people, for example, the kitchen staff would order food about two weeks in advance and start the actual food prep one week out. A smaller gathering, perhaps 100 guests or so, doesn't require as much time. The staff would order the food one week ahead of time and the food prep would start a few days prior to the event. Catering kitchens are similar to restaurant kitchens, in that the staff gets most of the foodstuffs and supplies from large distributors, but goes to local markets or specialty shops for specialty items.

The big day has arrived. This is when the catering team finally puts the itinerary to use. It's time to load up all the equipment, supplies and foodstuffs. Working from an extensive packing list, the crew loads vans and trucks with all the supplies. Nothing goes unchecked—the crew accounts for every linen, glass, chafing dish, tray, pot, pan and silver piece on the packing list. They even itemise small items like aluminum foil, saran wrap and garbage bags.

Caterers use an array of portable appliances and heavy equipment—ovens, fryers, hot boxes and dishwashers to name a few. For example, many catering services uses industrial convection ovens that have been put on wheels and converted from natural gas to propane for mobility. One tank of propane provides enough power for five hours of cooking time. Complete with burners for stove-top cooking, each oven cavity can accommodate four sheet pans of food. That may not sound like a lot, but at forty 8-ounce filets per sheet pan, that's 160 steaks!

The catering crew transports the supplies to the event site and unloads it all. If the site has cooking facilities, the crew unloads the cooking equipment (pots, pans, serving dishes, etc.) and food right away. Then they set up the tables and chairs, according to the precise floor plan. Typically, the client services representative or coordinator that planned the event manages all the setup work. Sometimes, the firm has to execute this front-house setup in concert with other vendors. This is where the detailed schedule, floor-plan and layout come in handy. Thanks to the detailed plan, the florist knows where to place arrangements, the musicians know where to set up their instruments, and so on.

For an outdoor event without cooking facilities, things get a little more interesting: The crew has to assemble a temporary kitchen immediately. The team divides the tents into two staging areas, one for presentation and serving and one for cooking. A hanging wall separates the two areas of each tent. On the kitchen side, tables line the outside walls and run down the center. The crew also sets up the ovens, hotboxes and other equipment. Hot boxes are large insulated steel booths lined with racks that can hold 40 to 50 sheet pans of food. The kitchen staff uses sterno cups, small cups of inflammable gel, to keep the hot boxes warm. Once lit, a sterno cup will burn for about 4 hours.

If the caterer is serving the food buffet style, the crew will set up stations with serving platters and chafing dishes around the event. The kitchen staff cooks and prepares the food and buffet attendants and runners keep the stations stocked. Sterno cups keep food warm and dry ice keeps food cold. For example, at a dessert station, the catering team will use dry ice wrapped in linen to support a ceramic serving bowl of ice cream. This prevents the ice cream from melting for three, possibly four hours.

Types of Service

Different functions call for different types of service. For example, for a cocktail buffet, the team at Joel uses this formula to decide what the staffing needs are:

— 1 Coordinator per event

— 1 Supervisor per event

— 1 Waiter per 30 - 50 people

— 1 Steward per 100 people

— 1 Buffet Attendant per buffet / station

— 1 Runner per buffet / station

— 1 Bartender per 75 people

— 1 Kitchen Manager per buffet station

So, a cocktail buffet for 150 people with seven buffet stations would have a service staff consisting of three to five waiters, seven buffet attendants, seven runners, one or two stewards and two bartenders. The coordinator or event supervisor meets with the service staff to go over their duties. Some will be manning the buffet stations, some will circulate through the event serving hors d'oeuvres and others will run food from the kitchen to the buffet and bus dishes. With everyone properly informed of their responsibilities, the event should run smoothly. Throughout the event, the coordinator continues to oversee each phase, making sure the detailed schedule is strictly followed.

The Clean-up

After the function is over, it's time to clean everything, break down all the equipment and tables and pack it all up to go back to the catering premises. The crew breaks out the original packing list to make sure they account for everything. As with every other stage of the function, the team has to execute the clean-up meticulously. The caterer's goal is to leave the space as clean—if not cleaner, than they found it. The team washes supplies such as glassware, silver and dishes and wraps them for storage. They identify and clean all rented supplies, and return them to the rental agency.

As you can see, catering can be an exciting career that requires creativity and excellent organisational and people skills. Let's take a look at what you can do to prepare for a career in catering.

Food safety

It is becoming all too familiar to hear of guests at private parties being taken ill with food poisoning. Sometimes food prepared in the home has been taken somewhere else to be eaten, such as the village hall, community centre, or social club where the function is being held. What should have been a happy occasion for everyone can turn out to be just the opposite for some.

Food poisoning is a miserable and potentially dangerous experience. It is your responsibility to ensure that your food does not make the guests ill. If it does, you run the risk of spoiling the function and alienating your friends. You also need to take extra care with people coming to the party who are specially vulnerable, for example, young children, pregnant women, the elderly and anyone who is ill. This information is directed at people handling or preparing food at home for family or friends.

A very wide range of foods can cause food poisoning if not handled properly. Raw poultry, and occasionally raw eggs, may contain food poisoning bacteria, and are often associated with food poisoning outbreaks. Meat and meat products, and fish and shellfish, have similarly been identified as culprits when illness has struck. Sauces and desserts like mousses and home-made ice creams, which may contain eggs which have not been cooked, may cause problems too. Likewise you also need to be careful with raw salads and vegetables which do not undergo any further process before they are eaten. Many foods can be a source of food poisoning bacteria - proper precautions must be taken in preparing them.

Common Faults

Some of the most common faults which may lead to poisoning are:-

— poor storage;

— cold foods not kept cold enough or hot foods hot enough;

— inadequate cooking;

— cross-contamination;

Storage

Large functions mean large quantities of cooked and uncooked food competing for limited amounts of fridge and freezer space. Inappropriate storage is one of the commonest faults reported as contributing to food poisoning outbreaks. Food is often left unrefrigerated for prolonged periods. Domestic fridges are not designed to cope with the large amounts of food prepared in the home for parties.

Don't take chances. Before you take on a task of catering for large numbers from home, make sure you've got the fridge and freezer capacity needed to keep food cool and safe.

In case there are any drips from raw meat or defrosting food, keep these items at the bottom of the fridge, below where any cooked food is stored. Protect the salad tray from any drips too

Keep cooked and uncooked food separate

Don't clutter the fridge up with wines, beers and soft drinks. While these drinks may taste better cold, they don't need to be refrigerated from the point of view of food safety. Keep them in separate ice buckets, cool bags or cold water so that you can maximise available fridge space for perishable items.

Temperature control

It is of course important to keep perishable food in the fridge, particularly if the weather is mild as bacteria grow quickly at temperatures above 10°C.

Remember:

— The coldest part of your fridge should be kept between 0oC and 5°C (32-41°F). Use a fridge thermometer to check the temperature.

— Don't overload your fridge. The efficiency of the fridge will suffer if the cooling air circulating within it cannot flow freely.

— Keep the fridge door closed as much as possible. Leaving the door open raises the temperature.

— Prepare food that needs to be kept in the fridge last. Don't leave it standing around at room temperature. Leaving food, which won't be heated again before being eaten, for hours at room temperature can be a recipe for disaster.

Cooked foods which need to be chilled should be cooled as quickly as possible. But don't put them in the fridge until they are cool as this will just push the temperature of the fridge up. To cool hot food quickly, place it in the coolest place you can find—often not the kitchen! Another way is to put the food in a clean, sealable contained, and put it under a running cold water tap or in a basin of cold water. Also, make full use of ice packs in cool bags. Where practical, reduce cooling times by limiting size of meat joints or dividing products into smaller amounts.

Once prepared, getting the food to where the function is being held can be a problem. This can be particularly difficult when there are large quantities of perishable food involved. Use cool boxes. Once there, are facilities adequate for keeping hot foods hot and cold foods cold? Adequate fridge and cooker capacity at the place where the function is being held is just as important as in the home.

Cooking

Cooking food thoroughly—which means making sure that the temperature at the centre reaches at least 70°C for at least two minutes—is the key to killing most of the harmful bacteria that cause food poisoning. Large meat joints or whole poultry need special care.

Make sure meat and poultry are fully thawed before cooking. The best way to thaw food is either in the fridge or by microwaving.

Make sure that the centre is well cooked. Cook until the juices run clear.

Use a meat thermometer if possible.

Domestic ovens may not have the capacity to handle the amounts of food needed to be cooked for functions, particularly if large joints of meat and whole poultry are involved.

Make sure çooked food is not reheated more than once. Always heat until piping hot all the way through.

Don't be tempted to cut cooking times just because people are waiting to eat. This is particularly important when microwaving or barbecuing.

Take proper care with left-overs. Throw away any perishable food that has been standing at room temperature for more than a couple of hours, and all food scraps. Store other left-overs in clean, covered containers in the fridge an eat within 48 hours.

Cross-contamination

Cross-contamination (that is, bacteria spreading from foods yet to be cooked, or from pets, hands, dirty cloths etc on to prepared food) can play an important part in food poisoning outbreaks.

Cooking for large numbers can mean more people in the kitchen at the same time. There are likely to be greater quantities of food, raw and cooked. Larger numbers of pots, pans, plates and utensils being used. More washing up. Greater problems keeping work tops clean. There are certain basic rules which will help reduce the scope for cross-contamination.

Prepare raw and cooked food separately. Don't use the same knife or chopping board for raw meat, cooked food and raw fruit or vegetables unless they are cleaned thoroughly in hot soapy water between uses.

Wash dishes, worktops and cutlery with hot water and detergent.

Keep your hands clean at all times. Always wash them in hot soapy water before touching food, after using the toilet, or touching pets, dirty washing or the dustbin. Hands should also be washed frequently whilst preparing food, especially between handling raw and cooked foods.

Keep dishcloths clean and change tea towels and hand towels frequently.

Make sure, if you have any cut or grazes on exposed areas, that these are kept covered with a waterproof dressing. Don't wipe your your hands on the tea towel. Use a separate kitchen towel.

Keep anyone who is, or has recently been, ill with diarrhoea or vomiting out of the kitchen, even if they're not handling food.

Vulnerable groups

Take extra care if babies, toddlers, pregnant women, or anyone who is ill are attending the party as food poisoning bacteria can make them very ill.

These groups should avoid using raw (unpasteurised) milk. This milk has not been heat-treated and may therefore contain organisms harmful to health. Make sure that are alternatives to pate and soft ripened cheeses like brie, camembert and blue-vein types for pregnant women and anyone with a low resistance to infection.

Catering from home for large functions is not something to be taken on lightly. Large amounts of food need to be prepared in advance and store appropriately prior to consumption. If not done properly the risk of food poisoning is increased. You need to plan ahead and think carefully about food safety.

Plan carefully

— DON'T make foods too far in advance.

— DO make sure you've got enough fridge and freezer space. Enlist the help of friends and neighbours to ensure you have the capacity you need.

— DON'T leave food standing around for several hours in a warm room before it is eaten.

— DO take special care with vulnerable groups.

Proper temperature control is essential

— DO make sure that perishable food is kept chilled. This means cold meats, quiches, desserts etc. Keep the most perishable foods in the coldest part of the fridge; but always store cooked food above raw, in case there are any drips.

— DO make sure that food is cooked thoroughly. Large meat joints and whole poultry need special care to make sure the centre is well cooked. If you're re-heating food, don't do it more than once. Always heat until piping hot all the way through.

— DO keep hot food hot and cold food cold.

Avoid contaminating prepared food

— DON'T let raw foods, like meat and poultry, or unwashed fruit, vegetables and salads, come into contact with food that is ready to eat.

— DO wash your hands thoroughly before touching foods and handling raw foods like meat and poultry.

— DON'T use raw eggs in uncooked foods, eg chocolate mousse, cake icing and home-made mayonnaise. Use pasteurised egg or commercial mayonnaise.

2

MANAGING BANQUET FUNCTION

Once the banquet manager has the information, it has to be transmitted to the staff in a clear, concise manner. Different banquet managers use different techniques for accomplishing this task. However, they all have one thing in common: every successful banquet manager has an organised system. Parties are served that have as many as two thousand guests. These guests are served in the same physical area where baseball and football games are played. In such cases, the banquet manager becomes the off-premise caterer.

Both facilities have a limited kitchen area and equipment to accommodate the large number of guests. The banquet manager must plan and organise the banquets, keeping in mind the limitations of both facilities. He or she also has the responsibility for obtaining all utensils and plates to feed the many guests. In addition, the banquet manager must obtain all the service staff to serve the guests.

Once a party is booked, the banquet manager should make lists of what they have to do for the event. By compiling these lists, he or she makes certain that nothing is forgotten for the event. Finally, the banquet manager must have everything the client has ordered and make sure it is served the way the client desires it. Another banquet facility, uses a more sophisticated process in the planning and operation of functions. Each day, the sales and banquet staff receive a computerised print-out which consists of five parts: deposits due, banquet event order (beo) due, guarantee due, personal thank you, and signed beo received.

Organisation is one of the keys for a banquet manager to be successful in this business. Both of the above individuals have a system to help them do their job. Without organisation, their jobs would be impossible to accomplish.

Once the client has reserved a date, the banquet manager must schedule an appointment to discuss all the particulars concerning the event. At this meeting the banquet manager will listen, then suggest and guide the client to make correct choices about the function. Included in the discussion will be the physical setup of the room, planning the program and time schedule, and selecting the food and beverage menu.

The banquet manager usually will offer suggestions to the client to make the party a success. Often, a client has a general idea of what he or she desires for the function. As banquet manager you must help with details of the event that the client did not think about. It is the job and the responsibility of the banquet manager to help plan the event so it will be precisely what the client desires within the limits of your operation. In order to do the job effectively, the banquet manager has to rely on the sense of hearing more than any of the other senses.

The banquet manager must listen carefully to the client. The banquet manager's mind cannot be thinking of next week's party; all attention must be given to the client. By listening to the client, the banquet manager can offer suggestions to make the party a success. A morning report form for a banquet manager. This comes from a computer printout that is obtained daily. It assigns tasks to complete concerning past and future functions.

Policy Sheet

Each banquet facility must have a printed sheet that lists specific policies concerning banquets. This policy sheet must be given to and reviewed with the client at the initial planning meeting. Items on the sheet should include: the length of time a room would be reserved; the cost of extra service staff and bartenders; how long in advance a function room will be set up; and the policy on deposits, guarantees, and contracts. The list can be as short as one page or, for conferences, can be several pages. With a printed policy statement, most questions are answered. This alleviates misunderstanding between the client and the banquet management. Part of a policy sheet. All banquet facilities need a sheet that lists the policies of the banquet establishment.

Function Sheet

When the banquet manager and client decide what is desired for the function, it must be placed on an organised written document. The purpose of this document is to have the banquet house give the client exactly what has been requested, when it is requested. Everything that the client and the banquet manager have agreed upon appears on this document. This document has many different names, depending on the banquet establishment. It is sometimes named the banquet event order or banquet stencil. Regardless of the name, the purpose is to list in detail everything that the client desires for the event.

Every banquet establishment must have a function sheet in order to successfully serve banquets. Function sheets are generally broken down into three main areas. The top third is information obtained at the time of the booking. Only the banquet and sales office employees need this information.

This is the area of the function sheet that is of utmost importance to the employees. In reality, it is their work order. For example, it specifies the exact time that all events are scheduled. The service staff can obtain the information needed to lay the place setting and cover from the function sheet; the chef will be able to calculate how much food to order based upon the menu and estimated number of guests; the kitchen staff has an exact description of the food that must be cooked and served; and the bar knows what liquor the client has ordered and when to serve it. In short, everything about the function should be written on this sheet.

Training your employees to fill out function sheets accurately and completely will avoid major problems and decrease the stress placed upon your staff. This area is completed after all the information about the event has been received from the client. Notice that the price includes the gratuity and the sales tax. The price area should specify all the charges. Some banquet houses eliminate this section on the copy that goes to the staff.

The only thing left to be completed on the function sheet is for the client to read, sign, and date it. At some establishments a separate contract is sent with the function sheet. At other banquet facilities, the function sheet is used as the contract between the client and the banquet establishment.

The following are the purpose of the function:

— The first thing that the banquet manager must determine about the function is the purpose. It will either be for a social or a business event.

— Most of the time the main purpose of an event is not to consume a gourmet meal. The food, even though it is an important part of the success of the event, is secondary to the purpose of the event. The banquet manager has to plan the meal to serve the guests quickly and efficiently so the client can begin the program.

— When the client is having a social event, the purpose of the party is to honour someone or something. It could be celebrating a wedding or an anniversary. It may be a retirement party, or a company may have a banquet as a reward to honour its top sales producers.

— Business meetings have many purposes. Some are held to introduce a new product. Others are held for the staff as a reward for a job well done. Other meetings serve as a sales meeting for the staff; while still others are actually used to sell a product to a potential customer.

— Once the banquet manager determines the purpose of the event, the room and meal can be chosen.

— Choosing a meal is important for both the client and the banquet manager. A meal has to be chosen that can be served efficiently by the banquet establishment, taste good, and meet the needs of the client.

The main part of the function sheet is an open-ended area in which the banquet manager writes exactly what the client desires. All facets of the event must be included in this area: serving times for food and liquor; colour of linen; a complete detailed menu specifying everything that was promised to the client; liquor service; and special instructions.

The banquet manager needs to discuss every aspect regarding the event with the client. This is a must for obtaining all the information necessary for running the function. The banquet manager should always listen to what the client desires and then offer proper suggestions based upon the discussion. Once the client makes the decisions about the event, the function sheet can be completed.

Types of Meals

Banquet houses offer three types of meals: the cocktail reception, serving drinks and finger foods; the sit-down served meal; and the buffet meal. The cocktail reception is beneficial for the client who wants the guests to mingle with each other. There is usually a variety of food and drinks for the guests, located at set places (called stations) in the room or passed by the service staff (called butler service). Many times a cocktail reception precedes a sit-down dinner. As a general rule, guests should have approximately five hors d'oeuvres to eat per person if the cocktail reception precedes a sit-down meal. If the cocktail reception is the only meal, the amount of food must be doubled. However, one fear almost all clients have is that they will not have enough food to serve all of their guests.

Therefore, the banquet manager should find out from the client the makeup of the group of people who will be attending the event. The time of day and the type of event also influence the amount of food that will be eaten. The banquet manager can then suggest the correct amount of food based upon the information provided by the client. For example, younger guests will eat more food than senior citizens. The sit-down meal is the most popular type to be served at a banquet. At this type of banquet, all guests receive the same meal, chosen by the host of the parry. Many times a client will ask if the banquet establishment can offer the guests a choice of more than one main course meal. This will depend strictly on the capability of the kitchen and the serving staff.

Because the purpose of a banquet is to serve the meal quickly, limiting the number of choices is a wise idea for the banquet establishment. If the client insists that the guest have a choice of food, offer a choice only for the main course and limit it to two selections. The number of guests ordering each choice has to be given when the guarantee is called into the establishment. The client will be responsible for identifying which guest gets which entree choice. The easiest way to do this is by having different coloured tickets for the client to distribute.

Also, it is a poor idea to have the service staff take guest orders on how food (such as steaks) is to be cooked at a banquet. Taking individual orders takes too much time for the service person and too much time for the cook. Imagine serving steak for two hundred guests! If the client wants the guests to have many food choices, then the best meal selection is the buffet. Buffets offer guests an enormous choice of foods and a variety of serving options. The kitchen staff enjoys preparing buffets because they have the opportunity to present foods artistically.

Clients have three service styles of buffets from which to choose. The first is referred to as the simple buffet style, where guests serve themselves. Service staff is only needed to clear dirty dishes. The guest obtains all food, drinks, and utensils.

The second, called the modified deluxe buffet, has waitstaff set up tables with utensils, clear each course, and serve guests beverages. The guests obtain all additional food.

The third, the deluxe buffet, combines excellent service with the opportunity for the guest to have a wide variety of foods. The guests are served their appetizer, salad, beverage, and dessert. They obtain their main course from the buffet.

A banquet manager can tailor a buffet type service to meet the needs of the client. The above three types of buffets are only a guideline to the style of services for the buffets. The banquet manager can be creative and mix up the styles of service to create a new style to meet the needs of the client.

Alcoholic Beverage Service

Once the client decides on the type of meal service desired for the guests, a menu may be chosen. Most banquet houses have preprinted menu selection choices. Banquet houses usually have separate menus for each meal period, as well as a separate price list that includes the cost of all meals. Using a separate price list, the hotel only has to reprint one sheet of paper, rather than print up an entire set of menus when prices change.

Once the client has decided on what type of meal to have, the next item to discuss is alcoholic beverage service. There are two basic styles of alcoholic beverage service that are used for functions. Guests can obtain their drinks from an open bar, where the client pays for all drinks consumed. The other option is for the client to have the banquet establishment set up a cash bar. At the cash bar, the guests have to pay individually for each drink that they consume. Of course, there are some functions where it will not be appropriate or practical to have a bar in the function room; so none is set up. At those functions, guests who desire an alcoholic beverage will purchase one from the bar open to the general public, in another part of the establishment.

Open bars have many different options for serving alcoholic beverages. Like the meal service, the banquet manager has to suggest the correct type of alcoholic service based upon the desires of the client. The banquet manager should be able to estimate how much liquor the guests will consume. This should be based upon previous experience with parties of similar groups. For instance, the average consumption at an event used to be two-and-a-half drinks per person per hour. However, this number goes down significantly after food has been consumed, because the guests are full. Another reason for lower alcohol consumption after a meal is the public's awareness concerning drinking and driving.

Because alcohol laws differ state by state, the banquet manager must check the liquor laws in the state where the banquet establishment is located. The choices of service listed below should only be used as a guideline. Each establishment must decide on its own policy of alcoholic beverage service based upon the laws of its state.

Alcohol Placed on the Guests's Table

In this type of service, each table is provided with some type of alcoholic beverage. It may be pitchers of beer or bottles of wine. It could be two bottles of liquor with the appropriate mixers (called set-ups). The client is charged for the number of bottles that are placed on the tables. The guests serve themselves.

Open Bar

In this service, guests order a beverage at the bar and are served by a bartender. They may have whatever type of liquor the client has ordered. Generally, one bartender is needed for fifty guests at a cocktail party, and one for one hundred guests after the meal has been served. With this type of service, the client may be charged in a variety of methods. The first is that the client pays for all bottles of liquor that are opened. Another way is that the client is charged for only the amount of liquor that is used. Another method is to use the public bar and charge the client for the number of drinks that have been consumed. The method that most clients prefer is a per person charge. This way they know exactly how much money they will spend for the event. Another method involves providing the guests with tickets which are good for a drink.

A La Carte Drinks

At some events, the client wants the service staff to take individual drink orders and serve them to the guests. This may be done at an additional cost to the client if the banquet manager has to employ more staff to take and serve drink orders. The main job of the banquet staff should be to serve the food for the banquet, not to serve drink orders.

Cash Bars

This arrangement may cost the client nothing. The guests purchase their own drinks. Cash bars bring in less revenue than open bars. Therefore, most banquet houses have a minimum amount of liquor sales that must be attained. If the guests do not meet this minimum, the cost of the bartender has to be paid by the client.

The banquet manager should attempt to convince the client to have an open bar, if at all possible. First, the open bar increases the profits of the establishment. But more importantly, an open bar contributes to making the event a success. An open bar does not mean that all guests get drunk; but it does mean that the client is hospitable. Guests attending a wedding reception or any banquet are more likely to be in a positive state of mind when they are provided with drinks than when they have to purchase their own. This goes back to Maslow's theory, the love and belonging stage. The client has invited the guest to the banquet. Guests should be treated as if they were guests at the client's home.

Guarantee

The guarantee and set pertain to the number of guests that will attend the event. Both of these numbers are written onto the function sheet only after the guarantee from the client has been given to the banquet establishment. The guarantee is the minimum number of guests that the client must pay for, even if fewer guests attend the event. Most banquet establishments demand the guaranteed number of guests 72 business hours in advance of the event.

Most often this system works well. However, some establishments have found that clients play a dangerous game by underestimating their guarantee. If they have 200 affirmative replies for the event, the client knows that the banquet facility will set up approximately 10 percent additional seats, so he or she only guarantees 180. This way, the client saves money if some guests do not attend. This creates a problem with seating arrangements (which is explained in the set information), because many times all 200 guests show up. Some establishments, to solve this problem, have allowed the guarantee to go 10 percent in either direction. Therefore, if the host guarantees 200, a minimum of 180 will be charged; but the room is set for 220.

Set in the Banquet Room

Once the guarantee has been given, the banquet manager decides on how many extra seats to set in the banquet room. Oversetting generally ranges from 5 percent to 10 percent above the guarantee. As the party becomes larger, the percentage of extra seats must diminish; otherwise, a banquet manager would be setting up two hundred extra seats for banquets at the Astrodome. Therefore, many establishments state on their policy sheet the maximum number of seats that will be overset.

The reason for oversetting is that more guests may attend the banquet than had been guaranteed. Another, more common, reason is that often guests are in groups of two or more, and do not want to break up their group. Therefore, the banquet manager sets extra seats because it is easier to set them before the guests arrive. Banquets are staffed economically with service people. If a service person has to stop what he or she is doing and set up extra tables, chairs, and covers, it is detracting from the event and almost always makes the staff play a game of "catch up."

The only time the banquet room is not overset is when the client has seating arrangements. With seating arrangements every guest is assigned a seat. Most clients want their guests to eat promptly and their program to start immediately. The banquet manager must be firm in allowing the service staff enough time to serve and clean up the meal. For American banquet service, it usually takes between one-and-a-half to two hours from the time that the guests are seated until the dessert and extra items are removed. For instance, if the party starts at 7 P.m., speeches should be scheduled for 9 P.m.

One of the most challenging events to plan for is the wedding reception. There may be a receiving line, pictures, blessing, toast, first dance, cake cutting, and bouquet and garter ceremonies. A wedding reception meal generally takes three hours from the time the guests sit down. Time must be planned for extra alcoholic beverage service if there are cocktails before the meal. Once the client has decided on all the details of the event, this information must be placed onto the function sheet.

As you notice, the banquet manager has specified everything that the client desires on this function sheet. The reader can see exactly what time the cake is to be cut and what time each course is to be served. This function sheet is set up thoroughly, even to the pink fan-folded napkins. Each function should have this type of function sheet. By doing this, mistakes will be kept to a minimum.

Once the function sheet is completed, the banquet manager must send a copy of the function sheet to the client of the party. Along with the sheet, a cover letter must be included.

Scheduling Parties

Many banquet operations have more than one banquet room. Therefore, they may have more than one party occurring during a meal period. The banquet manager should not schedule two events to take place at the same time. Instead, try to stagger the times at fifteen minute intervals. It would be great for the banquet manager to sell the clients the same meal items. If it is impossible to sell them the same main course item, at least give them the same accompaniments. This is another way to improve relations with the kitchen, and also it will make the parties run smoother. Remember that the reasons American banquet style service is used are speed and profitability.

The Function Sheet Distribution

The banquet establishment should set up a policy of when to distribute the function sheet to the department heads. This should be determined based on the amount of time needed to order the food and schedule the staff. Many establishments find that two weeks in advance of a party is a good time to distribute the sheet. Each department should receive its own copy of the function sheet.

In order for functions to run smoothly, there should be weekly staff meetings for the purpose of discussing all events. All specifics about functions can be discussed. The banquet manager will be able to explain any special requests that clients want for their event. Discussions can take place on any problems that occurred at previous functions.

Many establishments use this meeting to have a dress rehearsal of the meal for the upcoming event. At this dress rehearsal, the kitchen prepares the meal for the staff meeting in order to work out any problems. After the food is prepared and eaten, the staff discusses any potential problems that may occur with the meal. These weekly meetings alleviate problems and misunderstandings between the members of the staff.

The banquet manager must learn how to work effectively with the kitchen staff, and especially the chef. The secret is to treat them with respect and make them your allies. In order to make the chef your ally, always ask the chef if it is possible to comply with a client's special request about a meal item before you promise it to the client. Include the chef in the planning for special menus for parties. Ask for and use the chef's knowledge in planning events. Most importantly, introduce the chef to the client of the party.

The kitchen staff should always be told when the food is excellent, as well as when there is a problem. One of the most effective methods of encouraging the cooks to prepare excellent food is to bring the host of the party into the kitchen immediately after the meal. The cooks will look forward to this positive feedback. As a result, meals will always be prepared superbly. Communication and respect will make it easy to work with the kitchen. If the banquet manager does not have an excellent working relationship with the kitchen, major problems will occur at functions.

Checking

The banquet manager should check with the client three or four days before the event. At this time, the guarantee must be obtained from the client. This is also the time that the banquet manager must verbally recheck every item step by step to make sure there will be no misunderstanding with the client. The banquet manager must do this even though the client has signed the function sheet; the client may not have read what he or she has signed. If the client gives the banquet manager any changes, it must be communicated on all the function sheets. Whenever any written changes are made on the function sheet, they must be initiated by the person who made the change, and the department head must be told verbally of the change.

Arrangements of Seating

The banquet manager is often asked to help plan seating arrangements for the party. The following is a step-by-step procedure for planning seating arrangements:

1. The estimated number is received from the client. Give the client a tentative floor plan. The circled number is the number of guests to be seated at the table; the other number is the table number.
2. As the client receives positive responses, guests are placed in groups that correspond to the circled numbers.
3. The client assigns groups to tables.
4. After all guests have been assigned a table number, the client makes an alphabetised listing of the guests' names and table numbers.
5. The client does all the planning and writing of the names.
6. The client brings the alphabetised cards and list to the banquet establishment on the day of the party.

On the day of the party, the staff put table numbers on each table that correspond to the floor plan that the banquet manager has given the client.

8. On a table at the entrance to the banquet room, the cards are placed in alphabetical order. The guests find their names, read the cards, and proceed to the tables with the numbers that correspond to their cards.
9. The banquet manager should have the alphabetised list as a double check in case there is a problem with the cards.

Weekly and Daily Function Sheet

The banquet manager now has all the information for the event on the function sheet. In order to let all the staff in the establishment know what even are happening, the banquet office uses two forms. One of these forms is a weekly function sheet (distributed on the same day every week), which is given to all departments. In addition, an updated daily functions sheet should be distributed.

Both of these sheets should have all the events taking place in the establishment, not just the food functions. This allows all staff to be in the "knowledge loop." The daily function sheet is simply an update of the weekly function sheet. The guarantee is on the sheet.

Once all this information has been gathered, the banquet manager can proceed to run the party.

1. Organisation is the key to a successful banquet.
2. The purpose of the function determines the planning of the menu.
3. There are three types of banquet function meals: cocktail reception, sit-down meal, and buffet meal.
4. Buffets can be simple buffet, modified deluxe buffet, or deluxe buffet.
5. Alcoholic beverage services are: alcohol placed on guests' tables, open bar, a la carte drinks, or cash bar.

3

Waiter Service

A waiter is a person who "waits" on tables, often at a restaurant. A female waiter is often called a waitress, though the gender-neutral term "server" and collective noun "waitstaff" are gaining ground. Waiters' duties include preparing tables for a meal, taking customers' orders and serving drinks and food in a restaurant. Depending on the type of restaurant, this may involve other uncommon duties, such as singing a birthday song to customers who are celebrating a birthday. A theme restaurant may even require waiters to dance.

"Silver Service" waiters are specially trained to serve at banquets or high-end restaurants. They follow specific rules of service and it is a skilled job. They generally wear black and white with a long, white apron (extending from the waist to ankle). The head waiter is in charge of the staff of waiters, and is also responsible for assigning seating. This person can also be referred to as the maître d'hôtel. Some restaurants employ busboys to assist the waiters.

In the United States and some other Western countries, it is traditional to tip a waiter after a meal. In the U.S., waiters often are paid a minimum wage lower than the legally required minimum wage for most other occupations, as their income is supplemented by tips they receive. For example, servers in Georgia are generally paid around $2.13 an hour.

In contrast to this practice, waiters in many East Asian countries refuse tips, where they are sometimes considered an insult. Many cultures in the region believe that leaving a tip implies that the waiter is not being paid enough by his or her employer. Tipping is not traditional in Australia or New Zealand and is not factored into wages of waitstaff. However, tips are appreciated especially if the customer or party has been unusually difficult or has left a mess. Many parents of small children leave a small tip. Tips in Australia, because they are not a significant part of the income of the service staff are usually token amounts rather than a percentage of the bill.

Working Conditions

As a waiter or waitress you serve food and drink to diners at their table. Your tasks would vary depending on the establishment you work in, but all include taking orders and serving food and drink. Making customers feel welcome and comfortable is an essential part of the job. To do this work you should have a welcoming, friendly attitude, a good memory, a high standard of personal hygiene and should be well turned out. You also need excellent communication skills and basic mathematical skills for calculating bills.

Working hours vary, but usually include evenings, weekends, public holidays and shift work. Overtime, part-time and seasonal work might be available. You will be on your feet all the time in warm, often hot conditions.

Waiters and waitresses serve food in restaurants and other dining establishments. Depending on the size and type of restaurant, waiters and waitresses have a variety of job duties. Waiters and waitresses take orders for food and drinks. They describe daily specials and are sometimes asked to suggest an item on the menu or explain how an item is prepared. After writing down or memorising orders, waiters and waitresses relay orders to the kitchen staff or enter them into computers.

Waiters and waitresses serve beverages. If ordered, they serve appetizers, salads, or soups before the main course. When the main course is ready to be served, waiters or waitresses make sure the order is complete and may add garnishes to the plate. Sometimes waiters or waitresses carve meats or prepare special items at customers' tables.

Waiters and waitresses observe customers to make sure they have everything they need. They refill water glasses or other beverage items when needed. They also watch to determine when each course has been completed. Waiters and waitresses describe and take orders for dessert. They sometimes bring a tray containing a serving of each dessert special to customers' tables. When the meal is complete, waiters or waitresses remove the dishes and glasses from the table and take them to the kitchen. They compute the cost of the meal and prepare the check. They also accept payments or refer customers to the cashier.

After customers have left, waiters or waitresses may replace the table linen and service. They refill salt, pepper, sugar, cream, and condiment containers. They also clean and arrange work stations, chairs, and table pieces. In more expensive restaurants, headwaiters may greet and direct customers to tables. Headwaiters also take reservations over the phone and supervise other staff.

Preparation

To work as a waiter or waitress, you need:

— on-the-job training;

- excellent communication skills; and
- work experience in a restaurant.

Educational Qualifications

There are no formal education requirements beyond high school. However, some professional technical schools offer special training. Formal restaurants may require experience in food service. Informal restaurants are less likely to require experience.

On-the-job Training

Most waiters and waitresses learn their skills on the job from an experienced worker. Some restaurants offer their own training program. Training includes: job duties; and restaurant policies. Training may last up to a month. Following are examples of the tasks required for a waiter or waitress position.

- Check patrons' identification in order to ensure that they meet minimum age requirements for consumption of alcoholic beverages.
- Check with customers to ensure that they are enjoying their meals and take action to correct any problems.
- Escort customers to their tables.
- Explain how various menu items are prepared, describing ingredients and cooking methods.
- Inform customers of daily specials.
- Prepare checks that itemise and total meal costs and sales taxes.
- Present menus to patrons and answer questions about menu items, making recommendations upon request.
- Remove dishes and glasses from tables or counters, and take them to kitchen for cleaning.

— Serve food and/or beverages to patrons; prepare and serve specialty dishes at tables as required.

— Stock service areas with supplies such as coffee, food, tableware, and linens.

Basic Guidelines for Ensuring Good Service from a Cocktail Server

1. Learn the name of your waitress or waiter.
2. Know what your order is and tell it precisely.
3. Don't waste your server's time with small talk if she or he is busy.
4. Tip big on the first round.
5. If people in your party can't make up minds, order for them later.
6. Tell your server if you want your cocktail prepared a special way.
7. If drink is not right, send it back before it is half gone.
8. Let your server know if you if you have a special occasion. She or he may be able to have it announced.
9. Never touch your server in an improper manner. That is the easiest way to get drinks spilled on you.
10. Leave a good tip and make sure to thank server by name.

Tips:

1. Wait staff do give better service to good tippers.
2. Never argue with a cocktail server. The law is on their side and you've probably been drinking.
3. Never whistle or shout to get your server's attention.

Get Good Service from a Bartender

Here's How:

1. Establish contact, don't demand.
2. Know what your order is and tell it precisely.
3. Don't waste bartender's time with small talk if the bar is busy.
4. Tip big on the first round.
5. If people in your party can't make up minds, order for them later.
6. Learn the name of your bartender.
7. If drink is not right, give it back before it is half gone.
8. If you have a new joke, and bartender has time, tell it.
9. Never ask for a free drink.
10. Never pretend that a bartender is your servant.
11. Leave a good tip and make sure to thank bartender by name.

Tips:

1. Bartenders give preferred service to good tippers.
2. Never argue with a bartender. The law is on their side and you've probably been drinking.

American, French, Russian and Mangolian Service

The style of service that you choose depends on two things: the demeanor of the dining room and the demands of the situation. A formal restaurant is a more likely place for French service to be used, and having twelve people at a banquet table would be a good time to break out the platters for some Russian or butler service. While the basic tenets of each style are pretty well defined, there is some blurring of the lines between them-and some disagreement about which is which.

As the world moved into the Industrial Revolution in the 1800s, the world of food service moved quickly to fulfill the needs of workers. Factories drew large numbers of workers who had to be fed. The tight mealtime schedules caused a need for fast, efficient service. Counter service became popular, and the first Horn & Hardart Automat opened in Philadelphia in 1902. Fine dining wasn't dead, though. Delmonico's had a 100-page menu with 370 dishes and catered to New York's elite. In less than a century, fine food service went from being the province of the wealthy and powerful to being much more egalitarian and democratic. As Americans continue to seek out sources of prepared food, food service will become increasingly part of their lives.

This is a very popular style of service used not just in America but in many other countries. Its hallmark is efficiency, and thus it tends to be used in more casual and high-volume restaurants. Its efficiency has, though, attracted many purveyors of fine dining and led to its use in many formal restaurants. In American service, the food is cooked and plated in the kitchen.

The waiter delivers the food, one plate at a time, to the guests at the table, ladies first. These days, most service professionals agree that the guest should be served from the right side, with the waiter's right hand. Clearing of plates is also performed with the right hand from the right side. When the right hand is used for serving or clearing, the waiter should move around the table in a clockwise direction; it is more efficient (and safer) because the waiter is, by definition, walking forward rather than backing up. Conversely, any task performed with the left hand should lead the waiter around the table in a counterclockwise direction.

In most American restaurants, the service brigade consists of waiters, runners, and bussers. The waiter interacts directly with the guests and manages his or her station. Runners bring food from the kitchen into the dining room, and bussers clear and reset tables, pour water, refill bread, and assist the runner. Rather than threeperson teams, most restaurants have more waiters than runners, and more runners than bussers. This is because the runners' and bussers' jobs are more general and can cover more territory in the restaurant-their work isn't as guest-specific.

Originally, French service was used with meals that consisted of three courses, one of which was already set on the table when guests entered the room. Subsequent courses were brought into the room on silver platters and served from gueridons. Between courses, the guests would get up from the table and it would be cleared-not exactly a turn-and-burn.

While the current incarnation of French service is not quite as time-consuming as the original, this style has been relegated to the formal dining rooms of a few restaurants and hotels around the world. Not only does it require a large amount of expensive equipment, there is also the need for a highly trained service brigade to carry it out. This brigade is made up of the following personnel:

The captain almost never leaves the dining room. He or she is always in sight of the guests and is their main contact. The captain takes most of the orders, prepares the tableside items, and runs the station with the assistance of the rest of the team. The captain must have a profound knowledge of food and wine and be able to translate that knowledge into language that is understandable to each and every guest. As a mixture of salesperson, confidant, and advocate, the captain is the most influential person with regard to the quality of the guest's dining experience.

The front waiter is the captain's lieutenant. His or her duties include regular table maintenance such as pouring water and clearing plates, as well as assisting the captain with tableside cooking and tending to the guests while the captain is occupied, either at the gueridon or at another table. Occasionally, the front waiter will take drink or dessert and coffee orders, but the dinner order (because of its importance and intricacy) is usually taken by the captain. The front waiter helps to coordinate the delivery of food to the table with the back waiter; the same team does most of the table clearing as well. The front waiter's position may not be as glamorous as that of the captain, but the captain relies heavily on the front waiter's efficacy.

The black waiter is also sometimes called a runner, but the terms aren't exactly equivalent. A runner is someone who brings food from the kitchen anywhere in the dining room. A back waiter, though, is part of a team that is responsible for a specific set of tables and brings food from the kitchen to those tables. In addition to running food, the back waiter will assist the front waiter as needed, perhaps pouring water, serving bread, clearing tables, and the like. So a true back waiter does more than just run food; he or she is · responsible to the service team.

Busser or Guard is a position that some people, unfortunately, look down upon. Needless to say, the busser is an extremely valuable member of the service team and can be integral to that team's success. Primary responsibilities include basic table maintenance (bread and water), clearing, and the resetting of recently vacated tables. A great busser can lighten the burden on the rest of the service team, enabling them to concentrate more on serving the guests.

In French service the various staffers have to work as a team. Each member has both primary responsibilities and secondary responsibilities-for example, the captain will sometimes pour water when the front waiter is helping the back waiter deliver food to a table. The captain, though, should not be running food from the kitchen to the dining room unless the situation is dire.

The hierarchy of the classic service team works very well, but there are limitations. First of all, the restaurant has to be big enough that four-person teams can fit in the dining room. Second, the prices have to be high enough that all the members of a four-person team can make enough money to live on.

Definitions of Russian service vary, but the most common involves platters of food being prepared in the kitchen and brought to the table, with the server placing the food on the guest's plate from the left side with the right hand. Sauce and garnish are served either by that waiter or by another one following right behind. Advantages of this model include the relatively quick and personal service of hot food to a large number of guests. It also shows off the abilities of the service staff with relatively simple training.

One disadvantage is that servers have to learn how to use the service spoon and fork in combination as a sort of tongs. Also, by the time the waiter gets to the last guest at the table, the platter can start looking a bit ragged. Portion control can be a bit tricky, especially if a guest asks for additional food, leaving the waiter without enough food for everyone at the table. This rarely happens, though, so the other two potential problems loom a bit larger. These days, it is rather common for waiters in many types of dining rooms to use Russian service to place bread on guests' plates. Additionally, being handy with serviceware can be helpful when splitting menu items onto two plates for guests, either on the gueridon, on the side stand, or at the table.While it might take a bit of practice, the effort will pay off, at least in the form of confidence at the table.

Butler Service

Take Russian service and let the guests serve themselves from the platter. That's butler service. The service utensils are on the platter for the guest to use, and the waiter still walks around the table counterclockwise, serving to the guests' left side.

English Service

Essentially, it is Thanksgiving dinner in a restaurant. The food is fully cooked in the kitchen and sent out on platters to the dining room. The host carves the meat or plates the main course and hands the plates to the guests, who pass the plates around the table. Side dishes are sent out for the guests to help themselves, but the wait staff performs the other aspects of table maintenance. It would be used in a country club or some other venue where the guest wanted to mimic a home-style setting while still being waited on.

Family Service

Family-style service is quite popular in some value-oriented restaurants, and also in places where the style fits with the theme. For instance, some Italian restaurants feature large platters of food that are brought to the table, where the guests serve themselves onto empty extra plates. It is a remarkably efficient style of service that can make a lot of sense (and money) for you in the right situation. The waiter's job is made easier in a number of ways: the order is easier to take, the food is easier to deliver, and individuals largely take care of themselves.The kitchen is also helped by the fact that a table of four can be served with three large platters of food instead of four appetizers and four main courses-three large plates of food take much less time to prepare than eight single servings.

Family-style service can be used in other types of casual restaurants. Customers enjoy the chance to serve themselves, it can lighten the burden in both the dining room and kitchen, and it can lower labor costs. As you can see, house style can function in two ways-both as a marketing tool, to attract a certain type of clientele (for example, businesspeople, or teens out with their friends), and as a way of creating regular business, by enticing back people who feel comfortable there.

To be successful, any business must establish and maintain a consistent level of quality. On any given night, customers should be able to walk into a restaurant and experience the type of hospitality the restaurant has established a reputation for. In the restaurant business, as in any field from sports to media to manufacturing, reliability and consistency are achieved through training and practice.To take a very different example, in basketball a winning team will always have more than one player who can be counted on to score free throws consistently, especially when the game is on the line, and that sort of consistency is due almost exclusively to hard work and practice between games.

In the restaurant business, a successful restaurant has a trained staff who not only can manage an average night in a way that keeps customers satisfied but also can handle just about anything that's thrown their way, such as a large last-minute party with many special requests on a busy night, an equipment malfunction in the kitchen, even a waiter suddenly becoming ill and other staff having to pitch in to cover his or her tables.

Occasional flashes of brilliance are all well and good, perhaps drawing a lot of attention from food critics, but making quality a habit-establishing a routine so that every guest is greeted warmly within thirty seconds of entering the restaurant, giving waiters the information they need about the food so that guests'questions about the menu can be answered on the spot, making sure the dining room illumination and temperature are always at specified levels-is what brings customers back.

While, hospitality is a concept that depends on feelings and impressions, the essence of service resides in action. Service is being able to carry four dinner plates without spilling the sauce, or open-ing a bottle of Champagne without spewing foam onto the floor. Restaurateurs do these things to make people feel comfortable and attended to. While the tasks themselves do not involve emotion, they enable it, in the sense that carrying them out in a professional manner evokes positive feelings in guests.

Satisfying the instinctual need to take nourishment is the reason people eat. But why do they go to a restaurant to do so when good food is so widely available and can so easily be prepared at home? With over half of Americans' meals originating outside the home today, that is no trivial question.

There are many factors that contribute to the rise in dining out, such as increasingly busy schedules, greater mobility, and larger amounts of disposable income, but a primary answer is that dining out feels good: nice people bring you delicious things to eat and drink, and then wash the dishes after you leave. Restaurant folks take care of you. If hospitality is the final destination, service is the road map and the car.

Training for Good Service

The first step is to identify what feelings and experiences you want a guest in your establishment to have, and then determine what specific actions on the part of the staff will help to bring them about. A friend had invited a number of interesting people to dinner and spared no expense with regard to food and drink. Yet somehow the evening just didn't come together. None of the guests had ever met before that night, and the awkward silences were amplified by the absence of background music.

While the food was of very high quality, the various menu items were all very complicated and difficult to eat, and they did not complement each other well.The guests were left on their own to rummage through the fridge for any beverage other than water.

Every minute felt like an hour, and many guests seemed vaguely ill at ease. Some quiet jazz on the stereo, a simple bar with some wine and mineral water, and a few changes to the menu would have enhanced the experience, making for a more relaxed, convivial atmosphere that would have encouraged us all to get to know each other.

This, of course, was a home dinner party, but the lessons apply to the restaurant business as well. Specific actions can lead to desired feelings and emotions on the guest's part, and these actions can be singled out, defined, described, and put into simple, trainable terms-for example, anticipating the pace of a meal and bringing successive courses at just the right time, making suggestions of menu items that will complement dishes already ordered, and presenting the check at just the right time after the meal is done.

Many of the actions that can result in a guest's satisfaction are simple enough that almost any employee could be trained to perform them. For instance, getting your maître d'or host to address incoming guests with a smile and a greeting such as "Good evening". Yet getting your employee to do so with a certain level of warmth and desire to please-which guests will certainly pick up on, just as they will notice its absence-is not quite as simple.

You need to make sure the individual greeting guests at the door really enjoys contact with many different kinds of people and shows his or her enthusiasm appropriately. The hiring process for all front of the house employees should include a portion of the interview when the manager can get a sense of the interviewee's personality.

4

MANAGING CATERING OPERATIONS

A quality catering operation (like any other business) depends on how well all the little details are managed. Developing and documenting step-by-step procedures is always the first step in the process. Catering is a business filled with great amounts of constantly changing information. How well you manage this information will play a big part in how well you manage your entire operation.

TIME AND PLACE

In any operation, but particularly in an operation involving as many unique and disparate elements as a banquet, it is important to understand how each element affects the others. Planning decisions do not exist in a vacuum. A plan works or doesn't work as it fits in with the entire flow of the event. Thus, you must consider each aspect of a banquet, not in isolation, but in the context of its impact on all other considerations. In addition, banquets take place in real space and time, with real people.

You must take into account how your guests *and your employees* flow through the space and time of the event if you are to set up and service a functional banquet. Often, this piece of the planning process is the most difficult. If you could just feed everybody in the kitchen (off the prep tables, say) your job would be a lot easier. But clients tend to be picky!

The polished caterer is able to envision the flow of an event (from beginning to end) before the first fork is set. It is the ability to anticipate and plan for possible bottlenecks in the preparation and service of a banquet that is the key to pulling off a polished event. The old adage—put yourself in the client's shoes—is never more apt than in catering. You must constantly attempt to strike a balance between flash, function and financial viability.

Sales and Marketing

In general, everything that has ever been said about sales can be also be said about the art of selling a banquet. All the techniques that apply to selling software, shoes or hay apply equally to catering sales. While there are limitless approaches and strategies for managing the sales process, selling well is no real mystery. Much of it boils down to perseverance, organizational skills and a little bit of personality. There is no question that some individuals are just naturally much better at this craft than others.

It is often true in the food business that many who enjoy the art of cooking are not as comfortable in the art of serving. And some who enjoy serving clients are not particularly good at convincing them to make a purchase. So you must be sure that whoever is assigned the sales function is the right person for the job. Your sales staff must combine a pleasant nature, unbelievable patience, good administrative skills and the ability to convince a complete stranger to do things the way you want them done; at your price. Of these skills, the first two are probably the most valuable.

But generating sales in a catering operation is much more than just being bubbly and informed. In order to formalize the process of attracting and keeping clients, caterers must qualify and quantify their approach. Having the best food and service in the world means nothing, of course, if you can't get the customer to experience it.

Your Market

The first step in any marketing program is to do a full and detailed analysis of who your potential clients are in the local marketplace. Where are they located? Are they business or residential? Are they large or small? Are they high budget or lower end? Do you do weddings or Bar Mitzvahs? It is appropriate to get as much information as you can about who your competition is and what they are doing. The first order of business would be too simply call every caterer in the phone book and have them mail you a copy of their menus. Ask about what types of events they specialize in and what clients they have hosted recently. Understanding your competition better enables you to present your relative strengths and to play down your weaknesses.

Staffing

Successful businesses never lose focus on their people; they are far and away the most important assets of any organization. Without enough quality employees, even the best designed plans in the world will never come to fruition. The best managers are always recruiting, hiring, training, coaching, developing, promoting, and counseling. In the food service business, probably more than any other, turnover is constant, and if you don't look for employees today (when it appears you are fully staffed), you'll be short-staffed tomorrow, when two of your folks move to Phoenix, your best cook goes to the competition for fifty cents more an hour, and you catch your lead bartender giving away cocktails. On the reverse side of the dilemma, any organization that finds itself short-staffed with untrained, poor-quality employees, is doomed to failure, or at best, mediocrity. Without enough good people you enter the fight with one hand tied behind your back.

Recruiting

Unless your firm is quite small, recruiting quality employees must be part of your every-day activities. Too often firms wait until they are short-staffed and then by knee-jerk reaction post their un-noteworthy classified ad alongside the rest of the food service enterprises desperate for help. Attracting prospective employees does not solve your problem, but it is the first step in the solution. Here are a few tried-and-true techniques for attracting quality employees.

Setting the Room

For many, it is the design and set-up of the dining area which provides the greatest impact to the guests and the biggest sense of creative expression to the caterer. Indeed, setting an elegant room can make an impression that can last for many banquets to come. But setting a room properly, particularly when the size of the party gets much beyond a couple hundred, can also be more challenging than one may first suspect. Putting together a dining area which makes the best possible impact, while keeping the room serviceable, and more importantly, not wasting all your profit margin on set-up, is a task that requires good planning and years of experience.

Buffets Design

Buffet design and set-up can be one of the most creative

and impressive aspects of catering. It can also be costly, time-consuming and confusing. We will discuss several techniques for managing the buffet set-up process. Remember that within any plan, your food should always remain the primary focus.

Using diagrams

Almost all banquet operations make use of diagrams when mapping out a room set-up. Diagrams are extremely useful tools when communicating your plans to your clients and your service staff. Many operations have drawings of their most common table sets (with numbers or labels), to speed up the planning process. There is plenty of software available to make the diagramming process fast, fun and efficient. Once the actual table drops are finalized, one can arrow in the exact locations to place the food.

Remember that the table design flows from what is on the menu, and the table location flows from the room in which they are set, the number of guests, the timing of their arrival and departure, and the actual inventory of table shapes available. It is wise to know exactly how many of each type of table is available for a specific function. Never lose sight of functionality. Always walk the table set in your mind as though you were the guest. Be sure everything flows logically and naturally.

Creative Elements

Once you have determined the table locations, their shapes, and some sense of where the food will be placed, you will use your creative ability to create a stage on which to do feature your food. Some of the most common techniques in bringing to fruition creative designs.

Banquet Service

Your sales team attracted a client, first of all. They helped the client select a menu. They negotiated the final counts, the time and the place, the layout and the special requests; and eventually got their signature on the contract. Your kitchen staff purchased the food, planned and put together the prep requirements, cooked and dished out the food, while your stewarding department made sure everything was delivered to the right location.

Your banquet manager finalized the diagrams and planned the buffet set-up or table sets, figured out how much equipment was needed, made sure it got it to the right location, and set the room precisely as you (and the client) had envisioned it. Meanwhile, the beverage department stocked the bars and put them in position. But you're not ready yet. There are still a few meetings that must take place to be sure everyone knows their lines. Let us backtrack for a few important items before we open the doors.

The first order of business on event day should be a meeting with your captains to go over all the details. It is traditional to pass out copies of the Event Orders or Function Sheets. The banquet manager or supervisor should go over every detail of the functions to be sure the captains fully understand the plan for both set-up and service. A properly conducted captains meeting will allow your staff to proceed efficiently without having to stop for more information or instructions. It also enables them to answer any questions from the wait staff or your clients at any time during set-up or serve out.

Managing the Beverage Department

A large part of any catering operation is the serving of alcoholic beverages. Almost all firms set up a separate department whose duties are to order, store and serve all liquor, beer, wine and soft drinks, even if its only one person. Your profit margin on beverages is much higher than your profit margin for food. Thus, the caterer who can promote and manage an aggressive mix of beverage sales——alongside their food sales——will see better results on the bottom line. Alcoholic beverages, however, present many challenges for management that are unique to the product.

Storage and Ordering

Beverages should be stored in a secure room with limited access that maintains a consistent temperature (72 or slightly below), year round. You will almost always store your liquor, beer and wine in separate areas of the storeroom, and then sub-categorize within each category. Most firms will break it down a step further and separate their product by type (i.e. vodka, gin, whiskey, red or white wine), and then alphabetize within the type. Since some members of your staff will not be totally familiar will all the different types and categories of liquor, you may end up saving yourself valuable time searching for product if everything is in a simple alphabetical system.

Coffee Breaks

A big part of any in-house catering operation is the delivery and set-up of coffee breaks. It can account for a considerable portion of an operation's total sales and an even larger percentage of profit. While the basics of setting up a coffee break seem rather straightforward, setting a break properly—and within time constraints——requires an established methodology. In higher volume operations, where you might be dropping 30 or 40 breaks an hour (many of them with food), you must have a method that keeps the idea of flow in its proper perspective. Let us examine what it takes to win the battle of the break.

Establish Standards

Once again, documenting your procedures is an important first step in maintaining consistent quality with your final product. A few simple guidelines can go a long way. You must answer the following questions: Do you set your breaks left to right, right to left, or from the door in? Where do you place your coffee cups and condiments? Do you place food items before beverages? Are your cups placed before the ice and the beverages after? With china services, how many tray jacks should be set out, and where should they be placed? And the list goes on.

Staging

The key to managing a good coffee break operation is staging. By staging, the process of getting all the supplies you need in the right location, stored with some sense of organization, and then working from your BEO's to stage your services well before they are delivered. Coffee breaks are much like room service; you must leave the set-up area without forgetting any item you might need to properly service the BEO requirements. Forgetting something as simple as a spoon for the whipped cream can cost you a round trip to the cage, which could take another 30 minutes. Even worse than forgetting something on your way to the room is running totally out of supplies in the middle of a relentless rush. How can you prevent such a crises?

EQUIPMENT AND SUPPLIES

Keeping your equipment and supplies' cost in line is one of the most difficult challenges that any manger faces in the food service business. Equipment and supplies are difficult and time-consuming to inventory, constantly in use at different locations, and subject to breakage, theft, and incidental disposal. In high volume operations equipment runs a thin line between being an expense or an asset.

Like the systems you employ with your food and beverages, equipment should be kept in consistent, organized and logical locations. The process of always returning your equipment to the same spot makes it easier to locate for pulls and greatly speeds up inventories. In the same way (and for the same reasons) equipment and supplies should be secured when access is not needed. Even cheap silverware will walk if given an open door; not to mention real silver.

Making Profit

Keeping track of the financial aspects of your firm's operation requires the attention of every member of your management staff. Long before you turn the numbers over to your accountant (or accounting department as the case may be), you should have a clear picture of where you stand from a profitability standpoint. Let's start by taking a quick and dirty look at an example of a catering firm that is doing everything right.

Fortunately, most jobs in this world are not quite that complex. But you may find yourself (if you stay in the catering business for any length of time) battling challenges that seem as unstable and unpredictable as thunderstorms, and you may wonder why you put yourself in the pilot's seat. Few businesses challenge the full range of a manger's skill like the catering business. From an intimate, gourmet dinner for a select group, to a reception for several thousand, every event tests your ability to plan, communicate and lead. In the end, the difference between you and the competition comes down to details. Grand schemes and concepts are merely dreams. It is the ability to deliver quality food and attentive service that is the meat and potatoes of catering. To pull that off you must have a plan.

5

GUEST ENTERTAINING

Preparing for guests isn't difficult. The biggest problem is having enough space for everyone who visits. It takes some decorating ingenuity to make friends and relatives feel at home, but a few simple changes can make a guest's stay comfortable and enjoyable. Here are some tips:

— Buy inexpensive particleboard round tables (36- or 42-inch diameter) at decorating shops, home centers and department stores. The tables are easy to put together and can provide a space for three or four guests to dine or play games. Cover the tables with sheets, throws, large scarves or fabric remnants to jazz them up a bit. Complete by tying or attaching ribbons or upholstery cord around the makeshift tablecloths.

— Create additional dining or buffet table space by placing unhinged doors or boards across saw horses or file cabinets. Cover in the same manner described above and embellish as desired.

— Camouflage tables by layering the tablecloths. Start with a sheet that drapes to the floor, then add blankets, burlap fabric, canvas drop cloths or decorative fabric and remove any soiled layers after each meal to reveal a fresh tablecloth.

— Use large pillows on the floor for extra seating in family and children's rooms.Tossed on the floor around the coffee table the pillows make a terrific dining area for flexible guests.

— Use table and desktop storage units to hold china, utensils and other frequently used items so guests can help themselves and know where things are. A nice tabletop file box, in-and-out baskets, wicker office caddies and smaller items work great for allowing guests to help themselves to napkins, plates, coffee mugs and more. Also , any sort of divided basket or tray is nifty for placing utensils or snacks within easy reach.

— A wooden dish drain is another great place to put plates, glasses and mugs. It doesn't take up much space on the countertop and it's decorative enough to be placed directly on a buffet table if desired.

— For quick decorating, go into the backyard and cut attractive branches of berries and/or evergreen foliage. Spraypaint them gold, silver or even red. Add the decorative accents to houseplants or silk flower arrangements. A few branches in an old, interesting bottle can also be festive.

Arranging Guest Room

— Place several small bottles of water on the nightstand so guests don't have to find their way to the kitchen if they wake in the night with a dry throat.

— Make sure the guestroom is clean. Just because it was cleaned two weeks ago doesn't mean it's clean today. Cobwebs, dust and musty sheets are problems that guests will definitely notice.

— Place towels and extra toiletries for guests in a basket for easy transport to the bathroom.

— Remove any unnecessary furniture that makes the room feel crowded, but include a comfortable chair and reading lamp so the guest has a quiet space of his or her own.

— Remove clutter from the tops of dressers and other furniture to make room for guests' belongings.

— Clear space in the closet and drawers for guests to unpack. Provide a clothes tree for extra hanging room.

— Place a night-light in both the bathroom and the hallway to make it safer for guests to find their way. Also, place a flashlight on the nightstand so it will be handy in the event of a power outage.

— To ensure a well-rested guest, lay a foam egg-crate pad on top of the mattress for added comfort. If the mattress is old and sags, lay a piece of plywood underneath to give more support.

— To freshen a musty mattress, sprinkle baking soda between the mattress and pad. Let it sit overnight, then vacuum it up the next day. For quick fixes, spritz the mattress with lavender water.

— Throw already-washed sheets back into the dryer to freshen them up. Ironing sheets, even if they are wrinkle-free, gives them a crisp, clean feel. Freshen pillows by air drying them in the dryer with a fabric softener sheet.

— Add a down comforter with a duvet to the bed. To make the comforter look crisp and new, clean and iron the duvet. You can even change a room's decor by purchasing new duvets in various colours and patterns.

— Always have extra pillows (both down and synthetic) and blankets available for guests. Make sure guests know where they are.

— Other items to provide in the room include a nightstand with a clock radio, magazines , wastebasket, ironing board, iron, window treatments or shades for privacy, elevated stand for suitcase, a vase of fresh flowers, candles, a night-light, extra hangers and facial tissues.

Preparing for Guests

— Put together a basket of travel-size toiletries for each guest. The basket allows them to tote their items back and forth from the bathroom.

— Organizing expert Pam Hix shares tips and ideas on preparing for holiday guests.

— Let guests know what the holiday schedule is by placing an itinerary in a frame in each guestroom.

— Give out-of-town guests street maps of the city so that they can find their way around. It will help them and save you the trouble of having to give directions each time they go somewhere.

— Make an extra set of keys so your guests can come and go as they please.

— Buy new toothbrushes for each guest. It's always refreshing to open up a brand new toothbrush in the morning, and it's a pleasant surprise for them. Tie a ribbon around it for a decorative touch if you like.

— Make a list of where items are in the kitchen. Include locations of plates and glasses in the cabinets as well as where to find food in the refrigerator.

— For serving breakfast to casual close friends, simply go with the "help-yourselves" policy. Leave a note out where the basic items are kept in case guests rise earlier than the hosts.

— Serve a continental breakfast. Place milk and fresh orange juice in a bowl filled with ice, and serve doughnuts, bagels and pastries. Have plates, bowls and utensils laid out, along with some napkins and perhaps a toaster. Put condiments such as butter and jams in small bowls for presentation.

— A variety pack of cereals are a great idea for multiple guests. Go ahead and set out bowls, spoons and milk.

— Brew a fresh pot of coffee, or set up the coffee maker so that it is ready to go. The aroma of coffee is a pick-me-up and pleasant smell in the morning.

Guest Rooms

— A neutral colour palette and simple decor in the guest room will keep the room appealing to anyone.

— All the furniture in this guest room for the grandchildren was customised with the same paint treatment for a uniform look.

— A comfortable, inviting guest room lets visitors know they are always welcome.

— Guest rooms often are at the bottom of the decorating list, but they shouldn't be, since they are the one room your guests will remember.

— Since you are decorating the room not just for one person but for many, keep the design scheme simple. Be sure to include ample storage.

— When designing a guest room in a new home, you may want to position the room away from the rest of the family bedrooms for more privacy.

— The size and shape of the new guest room will depend on how it will be used, whether for long- or short-term guests. If guests stay a while, you may want to include a large closet and sitting area.

— Don't let the guest room become a repository for outdated or mismatched furniture. Try streamlining the look by treating all the furniture to a matching paint job, whether it is crackled, faux-finished, etc.

— A guest bath doesn't have to be as grand as other baths, but it can be warmed up with charming accessories. Good storage space, especially hooks, is an important and necessary addition.

Graceful Entertaining

— The more prepared you are the better. Start by setting the table the night before. Place the glasses upside down, and put out all of the serving dishes and serving utensils. Label which dishes go on each serving platter and then your guests can help you set everything out.

— Keep an entertaining journal with information on the meals you have served to your guests. That way, you'll never serve the same meal twice. This will also make a great keepsake. Take photos of your finished table and place in the journal.

— Keep a party box with decorations, candles, napkin rings, etc. Save extra decorative napkins for using when guests just pop in unannounced.

— Keep a cooler on hand for any items in the refrigerator that are in the way. These items will stay cool for a couple of hours.

— Relax for 20 minutes before your guests arrive.

— Wrap tiny boxes with little gifts inside and place in a silver or glass bowl. Let each guest take one home as a memento of the evening. This can also be used as the table's centerpiece.

— Always make guests feel as if the party couldn't possibly start without them.
— Insist that your guests sign a guest book before leaving.

For Perfect Guest Room

When you start to plan your guest room, think about what you'd expect to find in a 5-diamond hotel and try to make your room measure up to that standard. Your budget may not have enough in it to let you create a getaway oasis, but you can clear the decks, arrange what's necessary, and provide a quiet place to relax.

Following things to do or buy to help you set up a comfortable guest room for your visitors.

The Best Bed Your Money Can Buy

Don't give your guest the oldest, most saggy mattress you have. If you can't afford a new or good used bed, think about getting a quality air mattress. They're really quite comfortable and can be placed on top of a box spring, over a sofa bed mattress, or on the floor.

Bedding Upgrades

Beyond clean bedding, think about adding wonderful bed linens and comfort items often supplied by fine B&B's: a featherbed mattress topper, a choice of pillows, a cozy down comforter, extra blankets, and freshly ironed pillowcases.

Fresh Linens

Always have an extra set of bed and bath linens available for your guests. Accidents DO happen! Or you may have one of those wonderful guests who insists on changing the sheets when they leave. Let them do it! And thank them profusely!

A Place to Set Down a Suitcase

Clear a space to put a luggage rack or a small table or bench to set down a suitcase. No one likes to have to stoop over to the floor to pull out a clean pair of socks. Even a chair is better than nothing!

Clear the Decks

Resist the temptation to put your beautiful collection of dolls on the dresser or fill the closet with out-of-season clothes. In a guest room, less is more—more space, more comfortable, and more welcoming. Get rid of anything that you would not find in the room of a fine hotel. Keep only the most useful items in the room, like a clock and calendar.

A Comfy Place to Sit

Some people absolutely do not sit on a bed! And your guests shouldn't have to. Place an upholstered armchair or side chair in the room with a table and lamp close by.

Good Lighting

It's always nice to have a light control near the bed, so your guest won't have to stumble around in the dark, just to turn a light on. If nothing else, provide a good reading light near a chair or over the bed. Another fixture or lamp near the desk would be great. A small night light is helpful and a lighted magnifying make-up mirror is a real luxury!

Hanging Clothes Storage

If your guest room shares space with a home office, clear

at least a foot or two of pole space in the closet. Or purchase an inexpensive over-the-door hook that can accommodate some hanging clothes. Don't forget a supply of 6 or 8 hangers. A simple hook on the wall or behind a closet door can hold a robe, coat, or a purse.

Drawer Space

If you have an extra chest of drawers, how perfect! But at least clear out one or two drawers for small items. Both you and your guest will feel better with odds and ends out of sight.

Provide Privacy

You might know that the big maple tree just outside the window camouflages everything going on, but your guest won't. Choose window coverings that not only add to the character of the room, but provide privacy and light control, as well. If you must keep it simple, a nice blind can offer works great. You can always add a beautiful valance or side panels later.

Provide a Set of Keys

Put together several sets of keys to your home (and car if your guests will be using it). Colour-code the sets and keep track of who has what. Keep a simple log (where you can find it) of who has which coloured set, and check them in when they're returned.

Give Guests the "Inside Scoop"

If your home has a security system, provide instructions for your guests. This applies if you live in a gated community or neighbourrhood that has limited access to driveways, swimming pool, walking paths, parking regulations, or emergency evacuation rules.

Local Tourist Info

If your guests will be going around town without you, they'll appreciate area maps, brochures on the hot spots, and directions to your home.

Make a list of the best shopping areas, museums, parks, and your favorite restaurants. Mark special locations on the maps with highlighter pens. You can print out directions from major roadways and laminate them, making sure they know how to get back home! Place all the items in a box or basket that you keep in the guest room. You won't have to re-gather everything when another guest arrives.

Snacks to Stay

House guests get "the nibbles" in the evening, just like everyone else. Place wrapped snacks, fresh fruit or cookies and a bottle of water in the guest room. How about a small coffee pot or water heater, instant cider, tea, and coffee, and creamer and sugar? When your guests are up late at night reading that book that they can get to only while away from home, they'll be able to put together a tasty snack without sneaking down to your kitchen.

Good Reading at Hand

If you've read a wonderful novel, share it with your guest. Five-minute mysteries, travel books, an assortment of magazines, classic novels, or the local paper will provide quiet-time activities for your guest.

Center for Entertainment

A TV in the guest room would be much appreciated. Add a DVD or CD player and some of your favorite movies. Don't forget to place the remote control near the bed so they don't have to get out of bed to turn them off.

High Tech

If your home is wired, great! If not, provide a phone cord or cable connection to hook up a computer. Many people travel with laptop computers and love to do work or check e-mail when away from home. Provide a desk and chair and a good lamp.The list of things you've just read might seem very long, but the things on the list are very simple and logical to provide. By thinking of what you would like to find in a fine hotel room, you'll be on your way to creating a perfect guest room.

A Reading Light

Be sure to have good light in your guest room. But more importantly, have a good reading light that can be turned on and off without getting out of bed. A night light near the door and one in the guest's bath will be helpful and appreciated too.

Making a Good Impression

The first impression formed about a bed and breakfast home happens the minute your guest sees your inn and walks up to your front door.

The next impression occurs in the first thirty seconds when they are greeted.

Each owner has his or her own unique strengths and assets that can serve as a strong marketing feature. You must determine what these are and how you can best use them.

Entrance

Imagine you're a guest coming to your bed and breakfast for the first time. Examine the guest entrance.

— What mood does it set?
— Is it inviting?
— Is there a sign?
— Is the walkway clear and safe?
— Is there a porch light?
— Is it clear whether you should ring the bell or just walk in?
— Is the yard well kept and nicely landscaped?

The entrance provides the first gracious welcome to guests. If not, things get started the wrong way and it may be difficult to change your guest's opinion.

Bedrooms

Take an objective look at your guest bedrooms. Again, put yourself in the guest's shoes.

— Is this a room a guest will enjoy?
— Is the paint and/or wallpaper in good condition?
— Is the mattress comfortable?
— Will it provide good support?
— Is there adequate closet space?
— Is there a chair for reading and relaxing? It will save wear and tear on the mattress.
— Is there a desk or a place to write letters?
— Is there proper lighting for reading and writing?
— Is there a full length mirror available for dressing?
— Have you provided a night light and smoke detector in each room as a safety feature?

Expensive furnishings or special redecorating is not always needed. A new coat of paint and a few new linens may be all that is required. The room should reflect individual creativity.

Cleanliness

Probably the most important thing to impress your guests is the cleanliness of your hotel—their bedroom and bathroom.

— Are there cobwebs in the corners or behind the furniture?

— Is dust collecting under the bed?

— Furniture should be polished and dust-free.

— Drawers and closets should be free for guests' belongings.

— A scented lining in drawers adds a nice touch as well. Do be aware however, that some guests may have allergies or breathing disorders. If you fill your rooms with potpourri, candles and other types of scents, you may have some very sick and unhappy guests.

— A towel rack in each room may also be appreciated, especially if guests are sharing a bathroom.

— Are the curtains and draperies clean, framing shining windows?

If redecorating is called for, it can be done in stages as time and money permit. If you plan on redecorating, consider keeping a filing system with ideas, swatches of fabric, carpeting, wallpaper, and paint chips that can help you make selections in the future.

Ingenuity can be key to guestroom comfort. To expand limited closed space, a chest of drawers can be added, or attractive shelving with hooks can be mounted on a wall. A inexpensive round wooden table can become a nightstand or writing area.

Bathroom

Today, most guests expect a private bathroom. There are

some who won't mind sharing a bathroom, although they are becoming more and more rare. Carefully look over any bathroom that guests will use from their viewpoint.

— The sink, shower, toilet should all be impeccable. The importance of this cannot be overstated.

— There should be no unsightly mold or mildew on tiles, grout, around faucets or on the shower curtain.

— Mirrors should shine.

— Floors should be spotlessly clean.

— Be sure to include a wastebasket. Use a throw-away liner for more sanitary cleanup.

— Paper cups are more sanitary for guests than reusable glasses.

— Extra towels, soap, tissues and toilet paper should be easily accessible.

— Adequate lighting and high quality mirrors in the bathroom are a must for both men and women.

— Safety is also critical in the bathroom.

— A non-skid floor surface or rugs with a non-skid backing should be used.

— A non-skid surface or mat in the tub or shower is also needed.

— Check the temperature of your hot water to assure that no one will be scalded.

— Make sure that there is ample hot water for all your guests needs.

— Do faucet drip? This can be irritating to a guest trying to get a good night's sleep.

— After looking over your bathroom situation, a quick fix up with some fresh paint or paper and a few new linens may be all you need to start your bed and breakfast.

— However, if many of the basics are lacking, you should do some remodeling immediately. Do some research and use your imagination to come up with solutions to common bathroom problems.

— If there is too little storage space, consider hanging shower caddies or corner shelving.

— Shelving with pegs will add extra hanging space for towels.

— Some wicker plant stands can also hold towels.

— You may want to box in plumbing features under the sink and use louvered doors for a decorative effect.

— An old dry sink or a chest of drawers can be made into a working sink by cutting out a hole in the top and placing the sink bowl and fixtures in place. If you are handy and can do it yourself, you may be able to save quite a bit of money in the remodeling and redecorating process.

If the bathroom is shared, you'll want to encourage guests and/or family members to leave the bathroom in good condition for the next user. You may want to leave a nice wicker basket or some other attractive holder with cleaning supplies in sight. This hopefully will inspire guests to take a moment and clean up after themselves. If that isn't a strong enough hint, some type of clever sign can be used to get the idea across to everyone.

For Good Bed and Breakfast Host

One key ingredient in running a successful bed and breakfast is the ability to get along with all types of people who will be staying at your inn. When you operate a bed and breakfast, you become the host—not an owner—who greets and welcomes guests—not clients.

Hospitality is your business. A successful bed and breakfast operation builds its reputation on the hospitality it provides. Repeat business and referrals often come as a result of your interactions with the guests. Guests who frequent bed and breakfast homes usually seek the enjoyment of getting to know their hosts and sometimes develop close friendships with them. Bed and breakfast hosts can use these tips to increase their guests' satisfaction levels.

— Provide a warm, friendly welcome at the front door.

— Show guests to their room and give them an opportunity to settle in.

— If they feel up to it, you may want to give guests a quick tour of your home soon after they arrive.

— Offer a beverage and/or a light snack after guests have had some time to settle down from their trip.

— Be a "fountain of information" for your guests. As hosts, you should be able to answer questions about your area and mention nearby attractions and places of interest.

— Provide guests with a fact sheet listing frequently asked questions and answers about your inn and the surrounding area.

— Collect brochures and maps for the immediate area as well as other nearby areas of interest. Make these available to your guests at no cost.

— Collect menus from local restaurants. You may put these in guest rooms or leave them in your lounge area, perhaps in a three-ring binder, so that people may browse through them at their leisure.

— Offer "special touches" that will appeal to a variety of guests, such as offering breakfast in bed for newlyweds or for special occasions.

— Find out when guests arrive what they would prefer as a beverage in the morning, and always have coffee made early. A pot of freshly brewed coffee outside the door in the morning will be a treat for the true coffee drinker.

— Be sure to provide a variety of beverages so that guests can choose from a good selection. Coffee should be of the best quality—never instant! Experiment with different blends.

— Offer—for an extra fee—to make special picnic baskets for lunch or dinner so that guest may enjoy a special outdoor location. Be sure to look into your local food service regulations.

— Provide an umbrella stand with loan umbrellas near the door for guests who aren't prepared for bad weather.

— Set up a special corner in your public lounge area with a variety of games, cards, books and magazines. Provide a variety of reading material in each room.

— Have extra sample-size toilet articles on hand for your guests, such as shampoo, hand lotion, toothbrushes, razors and toothpaste. You can order a supply of many such items imprinted with your logo to promote your bed and breakfast.

— Use liquid soap or small, individually wrapped soaps in the bathroom so no guest has to use someone else's soap.

— A special guest "welcome tray" in each room can include fruit, cookies, or candy. Provide disposable drinking cups in each room as well as tissues, etc.

— Have an area which is easily accessible to guests where they can always find a beverage or snack of some kind.

— Keep an extra hair dryer, make-up mirror, curling iron, iron and ironing board available for guest use.

— Provide a local newspaper, as well as one with large circulation such as USA Today.

— Be able to provide your guests with a local map. Mark your home, restaurants and other attractions on the map.

— Collect discount coupons from local restaurants, fast food chains and other attractions for your guests' use.

— Leave a notecard or flyer telling guests where they can order a pizza if they wish. Let your guests know if it's all right to eat in their room or on your deck or patio.

— Make sure guests know that they should ask if there is something they need -- extra towels, more pillows, iron and ironing board, etc.

— Some hosts put together a collection of recipes to share with guests. You'll need to decide whether or not to charge for this.

— If you have a special hobby or interest, such as quilt making, invite your guests to watch you if they wish.

— If you have an historic inn, your guests may want to know more about it. Keep a scrapbook of pictures and documents detailing the history and/or renovations and restoration of the inn.

Restaurant Entertaining

— Offer to let the guest choose the restaurant. If the person hesitates, propose several alternatives, preferably with a range of cuisines, that you have dined in previously. This will enable you to be confident in the restaurant's quality and to make menu suggestions if asked.

— Make prior arrangement's with the restaurant's captain for a table placed in a desirable location to allow for privacy if you plan to talk business.

— Subtly arrange with the waiter to give you the check, make payment arrangements before you arrive or discreetly turn over your credit card early in the evening to avoid a possible "who-grabs-the-check?" debate.

— Even if you know what your guest plans to order, let him or her place the order himself or herself.

— Allow your guest (or senior or most important guest if there are several) to choose the wine, if applicable. Again, if the guest hesitates, if your knowledgeable, make a suggestion or ask the restaurant's waiter or sommelier to recommend a wine or wines.

Entertaining Spouses

— If you're married and spouses are included in the plans, once your guest has accepted your invitation, particularly for an at-home event, have your wife or husband extend a personal invitation to your guest's spouse or close companion. This will make that person feel truly welcome.

— If you have invited guests under the guise of a social evening, keep talk of business to a minimum.

— Engage your guest's companion/spouse in conversation. It would be ideal to find out a little about this person's interests, hobbies or occupation to start a conversation that will set them at ease.

— For social occasions, seat spouses apart to encourage lively conversation; preferably seating your guest of honor's spouse or guest by you and your guest of honor by your spouse.

— Choose several possible topics of conversation based on common current events such as movies, a televised special, popular books and the like in case of a lull in the discussion.

6

ORGANISING THE DINING ROOM

The individual who greets the guests is the key person in the dining room. This person may be called the maitre d'hotel, the director of service, or the host or hostess. Regardless of the name, this job must be staffed by a competent individual. In most instances this is the first human contact the guest will have with the restaurant. Therefore, the host represents the restaurant to the patrons.

Guests often decide to patronise a restaurant based upon the greeting and attention they receive from the host. The mood for the evening is set by the actions of the host. In addition to greeting the guests, the host is responsible for the operation of the dining room. This person is the one who must ensure that the guests have an enjoyable dining experience and must solve any problems that may arise in the dining room.

JOB OF THE HOST

The job of the host has evolved from the classical restaurant. In this type of restaurant, the job titles were as follows: directeur du restaurant; maitre d'hotel; deuxieme maitre d'hotel; and a maitre d'hotel de carne. This type of staffing had a host for each area of the restaurant. The directeur du restaurant had complete charge of the restaurant, including the kitchen and dining room staff. He was also responsible for longterm planning, food and beverage cost controls, and service. The maitre d'hotel was the host of all the dining rooms in the hotel. The operations may have been in many different restaurants.

The authority and respect of the host has deteriorated over the years. As service became more and more lax in America, the job of the host was considered an entry level position. Restaurant owners paid the host at the minimum wage rate because the owners felt that this person did not directly produce money as a service person. Consequently, the person who was given this job was poorly trained, if trained at all.

This position changed from being a job of prestige, power, and respect, into a job that restaurant owners felt anyone could do. Instead of having experienced waitpeople striving to become the host, they avoided it because it did not pay as much money as their tipped position. Guest service and the industry suffered tremendously. Today, the pendulum has begun to swing back to the experienced and respected host. Restaurant owners are realising the importance of

A well-informed and personable individual holding the job of host will make the restaurant a success. Restaurant owners are now compensating their hosts at a higher pay rate than the minimum wage. As the laws regarding tip reporting and taxes become more stringent on restaurant owners, more and more are instituting a fixed service charge. From this fixed service charge, the host is being paid a much higher wage than minimum. Other restaurants, which still have a voluntary tipping policy, make the service staff contribute part of their tips to the host. Restaurant owners are, once again, realising the importance of having a competent, personable host to greet their guests.

Selection Procedure

Selecting a person for the host's job is important and challenging for the manager or owner of the restaurant. This is because a major portion of the job is dependent upon the host to observe a situation or problem, weigh the positive versus the negative aspects, and make a decision-all in a few seconds. Because the ability to think quickly and react to situations positively is a necessary qualification, the manager must try to select an individual who is personable and can work well under stress. The selection process should be structured in such a manager as to determine the personality of the applicants and how they handle stressful situations.

Qualifications

The individual selected to be a host must:

1. Be personable
2. Work wellunderstress
3. Be able to think quickly
4. Be able to make decisions

The qualifications for a host fall into two general categories: physical and behavioural. The first relates to the appearance of the individual. The second refers to the manner in which a person interacts with people.

The host is the first person guests see when they walk into a restaurant, therefore the physical appearance of the host must be positive. This host makes a positive physical appearance. As with the service staff, cleanliness is essential. Any uniform (tuxedo or evening gown) must be neat and clean. These uniforms are a symbol of professionalism. The host should be proud of wearing the uniform.

The second qualification, behavioural, is the ability to deal with people. The host has to be able to meet the needs of the restaurant's guests and employees. Sometimes this is not easy. Many guests are not pleasant, because they may be having a bad day, are not used to waiting for a table, or for a myriad of reasons that the host has little, if any, control over. Employees provide another challenge. They will complain about the amount of tips that the guests have left and about their stations, for example. The host must have the ability to satisfy all the employee and guest complaints, whether they are legitimate or not.

For the host to do the job effectively, other behavioural traits are needed. The professional host lists some of them as attentiveness, courteousness, dependability, economy, honesty, knowledge, loyalty, preparedness, productivity, quietness, sensitivity, tact, persuasiveness, and skill.' Even though it would appear that every person has the common sense to know and use these traits, many do not. The following information will give examples of the importance of the specific traits.

Attentiveness

Like the service staff, the host must be ubiquitous. He must know what is occurring in the dining room at all times, and must appear to have eyes in the back of his head. The host has to know the status of all tables at all times; whether table 3 has been served the main course; if table 5 needs more wine. An absent-minded person or daydreamer does not belong in the position of host. This job requires a person who will be consistently alert to the guests' needs.

Courteousness The host must treat the guests as though they were guests in his or her home. Words such as "please" and "thank you" are thought by many people to be magic words. Guests appreciate hearing these magic words, and the host is encouraged to use them whenever appropriate. Greeting the guests by name and addressing the guests by name throughout the dining experience, the host should return to the table to show his genuine concern about their satisfaction.

By using the magic words "please," "thank you," "excuse me," and especially the guest's name, the host will not only impress the guest by his courtesy but will provide a positive model for the service staff to follow. Courteousness also includes assisting guests with little things that show concern. These little things are not something that will make a person jump up and down and say, "Wow, did you see what the host did!" Instead, they are displays of courteousness that will make the guests feel that the restaurant really cares about them and is happy to receive their business.

Examples of courteousness are: assisting guests in removing or putting on their coats; pulling out the chairs for guests as they are shown to their table; and checking back with guests to determine if the table or temperature of the room is pleasing. Pulling the shades down so the sun will not shine in the guests' eyes is another example. The difference between a great restaurant and a good restaurant is taking care of the details and courteousness is a detail.

Dependability

Dependability is a trait that is valued highly by restaurant owners. It is a sign of maturity. Basically, it means that the employees will be responsible for their own actions. It also includes the fact that the employees will accomplish the goals that have been set, either by management or by the employees themselves on their own without needing to be checked on. This trait is important in all positions, but is extremely critical for any person who will hold the responsible job of host.

Economy

Economy means keeping costs at a minimum. This will be the host's responsibility. The dining room is an area where costs can rapidly get out of control because of improper scheduling, improper use of linen, and food waste. If the host schedules too many service staff, the labour cost will be a drain on the restaurant. If staff are allowed to use extra equipment (like extra sidetowels) when they are not needed, money is lost. Common sense is important in keeping waste to a minimum. An example of economy is to save and reuse individual packaged jellies if they have not been opened.

Efficiency

Efficiency means fording the quickest and easiest way to do a task without jeopardising the guests' satisfaction. The ability to organise reservations in a systematic manner is an example of efficiency. By having an efficient reservation system, the host can take reservations correctly. This will allow the host to spend more time in the dining room (or working the floor) instead of trying to straighten out a mess caused by an inefficient reservation system. The more organised the host is, the more time can be spent with the guests.

Honesty

A person who deals with the public, especially in the host's job, will have to make many decisions that will test his honesty. For example, a guest approaches the host and asks for a table. The host has all the tables reserved and informs the guest of this. The guest produces a $50 bill and asks, "Are you sure?" The host and the guest both know that the patron is buying the table. What should the host do? Other opportunities will arise to deceive the customer as well as the employees. In all instances, if the host is dishonest and allows the staff to be dishonest, word will spread that the establishment is dishonest. This will result in negative word of mouth from both guests and employees, and the business will suffer.

Loyalty

Loyalty is another highly rated behavioural trait of a host. It can be defined as being (or giving the impression to the public of being) totally supportive of the ideas and philosophies of the restaurant. An example of not being loyal is downgrading the establishment to the guests by such comments as, "Management has no idea of how to run this place."

Knowledge

As with the service staff, the host has to know all facets of the operation of the restaurant. In fact, he must know more about the operation than the service staff, because the guests perceive the host as the key figure in the restaurant. The host should know all the facts about the operation of the restaurant, including the preparation and service of food and beverage. In addition, the host has to be aware of the physical layout of the restaurant, how to deal with credit card charges, and the accounting procedures of the restaurant. With today's ever changing technology, knowledge of computers and computer systems is critical.

Knowledge of community events and area attractions is an important part of the host's concern. If a guest asks a question and the host doesn't know the answer, he or she will have to find out the answer and return to the guest with it.

Preparedness

Nothing is more frustrating for guests than to have to wait for something: a reservation, food, or drinks, The host has to be ready to accept guests into the dining room at its stated opening time. If a guest is promised a 3 P.m. reservation, then the table should be ready for them at 3 P.M. Preparedness is the act of planning and organising all equipment and supplies so the guest will not have to wait for service. Procrastinators do not belong in the hospitality industry. The host should have a plan for each situation and be considering alternative plans in case of a problem.

Quietness

A good host is always available when needed. However, the host has to be aware of the proper time to talk to guests and when to leave them alone. When talking to the guests, it is done in a nice manner, not in a loud or boisterous one. The host must act with dignity, and do the job quietly.

Sensitivity

Restaurants are where many special occasions are celebrated, such as engagements, wedding anniversaries, births, and job promotions. Unfortunately, it is also the place where many marriages and relationships are ended. People often choose a restaurant in which to tell their spouse or lover that the relationship is finished, because they think that the hurt party will not make a scene in so public a place. The host has to be sensitive to the needs of the guests and observe their actions to determine how much attention they want from the host. Sensitivity is a two-part trait: first to observe what is occurring between the guests or to the guests, then act appropriately. If the guests have just become engaged, congratulations should be offered. A dessert or drink may be offered, compliments of the restaurant. If the couple obviously is having a fight, then staying away from the table is best. Going to the table asking how the food is would not be appropriate. That would show a lack of sensitivity.

Skill

A skillful host knows how to "work the floor." He knows how to obtain the most efficient or effective use of the tables in the shortest period of time. The skillful host knows how to keep the guests happy and how to motivate them to return. Skill also involves making salads tableside, carving meats and poultry, and pouring wine.

Tact

The ability to say the right phrase at the right time without offending the guest would be a definition of tact. Saying to a guest, "Where have you been, I haven't seen you in a long time," can be interpreted by many guests as tactless. A more tactful way of saying this would be, "It's nice to have you patronise the restaurant, we're glad to have you here again." This says the same thing, but it will not offend the guest.

Tact is also involved when inquiring about the guests or their families. The host has to be aware of what is happening in the community. Reading the local newspapers will give the host information needed to avoid embarrassment and appearing tactless.

Productivity

Productivity is defined as the ability to get the maximum amount of tasks accomplished in the shortest period to time. There are times when the host must take reservations, greet guests, take their orders, and return to their table to see if the meal is to their satisfaction. In addition, the host must monitor the service staff's performance, seeing that the sidework is being done and that the dining room is operating to its maximum potential.

Persuasiveness

This is another important behavioural trait, especially when dealing with guests who have problems. Persuasiveness could he used to convince the guest to take a different table, or to take a different time because the restaurant is sold out (booked solid). Convincing the guest to change his or her mind about something requires persuasiveness. There are many more behavioural traits that the reader will be able to identify; however, an individual has to exhibit some, if not all, of the traits stated above in order to be an excellent host.

Responsibilities of Hosts

In order for any restaurant to run efficiently, the host must be prepared. The key to having a successful restaurant or banquet are the five Ps of management: *Prior Planning Prevents Poor Performance.*

This phrase and the meaning of it are important for all restaurant employees. However, this philosophy is especially critical in the host's job. The five Ps of management mean that if all tasks are planned in advance, problems will be kept to a minimum. Therefore, a plan is needed to use before each meal period. By completing it, the host ensures that the restaurant is prepared to accept guests.

The following are some examples of what items may be on the checklist and why they are important. The list should include checking both the men's and ladies' room for all paper products and for cleanliness. If the host does not do this, it will have to be attended to during a busy time, taking valuable time away from the guests. Another important area to check is the physical cleanliness of the dining room. Are the floors free of crumbs or lint? If the floor is dirty, it will have to be cleaned or vacuumed before the guests arrive. All light fixtures are inspected for burned out bulbs or cobwebs. The host may think "It's not my job," but the host is responsible for the operation of the dining room. The guests want to feel that they are eating in a clean and safe restaurant. Burned out light bulbs, dirty floors, and cobwebs send a message to the guest that the restaurant does not care about cleanliness.

Checklist for Opening the Dining Room

1. Inspection of the service staff for proper grooming guidelines.
2. Men's room and Ladies' room
3. Physical cleanliness of the dining room:
   — Floor free of crumbs and lint
   — Light fixtures clean and no burned out bulbs
4. Printers have enough paper to complete meal period
5. Menus are clean and chef's creations have been added
6. Reservations have been blocked
7. Computer system has been programmed with the chef's creations
8. Host is neat and clean, ready to accept guests

For restaurants with a computer system, printers have to be checked first thing to see if there is enough paper to last though the meal period. With some computer systems, if the paper runs out, the computer will not work. All prices and new items should be put into the memory of the computer before the staff take their first orders.

The host may assign an employee to complete any task not completed. The first responsibility of the host is to prepare the dining room to accept guests. The host must have the dining room ready to accept guests when it is scheduled to open its doors. As has been said before, the difference between a good and a great restaurant is attention to details. A good host will anticipate and avoid problems. A great host will use the five Ps of management to have an excellent restaurant.

Knowledge of the menu, pricing, ingredients, and all facts essential to the smooth and profitable operation of a restaurant is as essential to the host as it is to the service staff. In addition, the host has to supervise the service staff. The host is responsible for making the service excellent. Successful restaurants constantly evaluate service throughout an employee's career. The host is responsible for the training and performance of the service. In addition, the host has to schedule employees and assign stations and sidework to make the dining room operate at its maximum efficiency.

Affected Factors for Scheduling

Have you ever been to a restaurant where you are served slowly because there are too many guests and not enough staff? Sometimes there is an obvious shortage of service staff to serve the guests. For example, a restaurant has 120 seats filled and only two service persons to tend to the guests. The person responsible for scheduling has not scheduled enough service staff to meet the demand. The host must schedule the correct amount of staff to meet the demands of business, while not over-staffing the restaurant. Overstaffing causes a loss of money and, at times, even results in poor service. In order to schedule effectively, the host must take certain factors into consideration and then schedule the employees correctly. The first step begins with forecasting.

Forecasting

Forecasting is planning for anticipated business based upon previous history of the restaurant, reservations, and events that are planned for the community which will affect the business. A formal written forecast of covers produced on a weekly basis is the most important aspect in scheduling.

Scheduling

There are many factors that affect correct scheduling. The first has to do with the qualifications of the individual waitpeople. The next has to do with the type of menu and style of service that the restaurant offers. The third involves events occurring in the community in which the restaurant is located. If the restaurant is located in a hotel, expected occupancy rates of the hotel will play a major part in scheduling. Another factor is based upon the history from previous years' business. The final factor would be the number of reservations from the meal period. Scheduling is one place where the five Ps of management are extremely important.

The first consideration is the qualifications of the individual wait-people. For example, one service person may be able to work best waiting on a lot of small parties; another may work better with large parties. Knowing this information allows the host to compensate for the inadequacies of the staff.

Next, the host has to consider the type of menu and the style of service offered by the restaurant. If the restaurant uses American service, the number of guests that can be served efficiently by one service person is anywhere from sixteen to twenty-four. Individual restaurants determine how many guests a service person is required to serve. This depends on the menu, the meal period, and the atmosphere of the restaurant. The host can use this standard in forecasting and scheduling.

The third factor that affects scheduling is events occurring in the community that will positively or negatively affect the restaurant's business. For example, if there is a parents' weekend at the local college, and the restaurant serves breakfast, then it should be staffed to accommodate extra guests. If there is a youth sporting event scheduled in the community, and the restaurant appeals to that market, it will be busier than usual. The host, the service staff, and the cooks want to avoid surprises. No one likes to be swamped with business when they are not prepared to handle it.

Work Schedule of the Employees

Based upon the factors that were discussed above, the host can determine haw many service people are needed for a certain time period. This time period is usually a week. It is beneficial to the host and employees to have the work schedule completed and posted in advance. This lets all employees know when they are scheduled to work. The restaurant industry has a reputation for not treating its service staff decently. Many times, restaurant owners engage in day-to-day scheduling.

When service persons ask for their schedules, they are told to call at 10 A.M. the next day. Then they are told to work or not to work. This type of scheduling is bad, because it negatively affects morale. Posting the schedule on the same day every week for the same period of time will alleviate the problem. The busiest days in the restaurant business are the times when everyone else is enjoying themselves (weekends and holidays).

Employees should be told when hired that they will have to work weekends and holidays. However, the host should strive to give his employees two days off in succession. There is a system the author designed in order to improve scheduling, and that resulted in improved morale. First, the schedule was made every Wednesday and posted every Thursday. As an example, the schedule went from Friday, April 1, to Sunday, April 10. The employees would know a week in advance who had to work the following weekend. The next week's schedule went from Friday, April 8, to Sunday, April 17. Using this method, the host is planning for seven days, but always scheduling for ten days.

This method improves morale and it will allow the employees to plan in advance if there is a special event they wish to attend.

In addition, if the employees wanted a special day or weekend off, they were allowed to switch with other employees, as long as the host was told. However, it was made clear to the employees who were scheduled to work that they were responsible for covering the shift. If their replacement did not show up, then the originally scheduled employee would pay the consequences. This system made the host's job easy. The staff was motivated because they knew' exactly when they had to work and knew that they could take a day off if some special event occurred. Of course, if employees knew far enough in advance before the schedule was to be made up that they needed a day off, they would inform the host and they would be accommodated.

Stations and Sidework Responsibilities

Regardless of how the stations are arranged in the restaurant (team or individual), stations and sidework responsibilities have to be posted. Sidework should be with the station. The host must be flexible, and on occasion must combine stations or service staff from different stations when it would benefit the guests. For example, a party of twelve went to a restaurant on New Year's Day. The host assigned two service people to take care of the table, even though it was on one station. The group was served more quickly than if one person had served them.

Menus and Guests Checks

The host is usually responsible for making sure the menus are clean and ready to distribute to the guests. In some establishments, the host has to write (or type) and put the daily specials into the menu, and/or write them on the blackboard. When putting the specials into the menus, the host also checks the condition of the menus. Dirty, torn, or smudged menus should be discarded. If the restaurant serves three meals a day, the host checks that the menu is correct for that meal period. Have you ever received a menu that was for lunch when the other guests in your party had a dinner menu?

Inspection of Staff and Daily Meeting

Before each meal period, the host has to conduct a staff inspection and hold a daily meeting. It is at this time that the host inspects the employees regarding the grooming and cleanliness policies set by the restaurant. If a member of the staff does not meet the grooming standards that have been set, the host cannot allow that individual to work. Allowing a service person to work who has not met the restaurant's standards will make it difficult to enforce the rules to the other staff members. Making exceptions will create problems with the other members of the staff. Once the service staff realise that the grooming and cleanliness policies will be enforced, they will comply.

The daily meeting usually consists of a short information session that the host conducts before each meal period. Information is shared with the staff, such as the description and price of the day's chef's creations. Any new wines or beverages that the restaurant is featuring will be explained. The soup or vegetable of the day and items that the restaurant is temporarily out of are also communicated by the host. Any special requests from the reservations and any items such as new promotions are also explained.

This informational session should not last long. There will be regularly scheduled meetings for the purpose of tasting food and wine, reviewing policies in depth, and soliciting new ideas from the staff. This meeting is only informational in nature, so that the dining room runs smoothly for that particular meal period.

7

Organising Dining Services

The host is a key player in a restaurant's moment of truth. Many times, the first employee of the restaurant who comes in contact with the guests is the host. The host may also be responsible for training and managing the service employees in the dining room. The service staff have many moments of truth with the guests. Karl Albrecht states that there are seven deadly sins concerning service. Being aware of them and of how to prevent them is the obligation of both the host and the service staff. The seven deadly sins of service are: apathy, the brush-off, coldness, condescension, robotism, rule book excuses, and the runaround.

Apathy: Apathy can be described as a lack of emotion or interest. An example of an apathetic host is found in the following example: The guest enters the restaurant and sees the host standing at the host's desk (the podium). The host does not acknowledge the guest's presence. Instead, the host appears to be interested in reading something that is much more important than greeting the guests. To avoid the sin of apathy, greet guests immediately when they enter the restaurant. Studies have shown that the impression made in the first thirty seconds of contact between the guest and the restaurant determines the feeling of the guest about the total dining experience. This is the first moment of truth for the restaurant. The host can create a positive one by greeting the guest within thirty seconds of arrival.

The Brush-off: Brush-off is a slang term that means rebuff, according to The Random House Dictionary.' Relating it to the host's job, an example of brushing off the guest occurs in the following cases: The guest approaches the host and asks (usually in a timid manner), "When will my table be ready? You told me it would be ready now and it isn't." The host replies, "In a few minutes," and walks away from the guest without any explanation or comment. The second moment of truth has been negative for the restaurant.

To prevent committing the second sin, the host should strive to give the guest undivided attention. To avoid brushing off the guest, the host could apologise to the guest and assure the guest that the party will be seated as soon as possible. The host will then seat that party when the next table is available. If the problem persists and a table is not ready, it becomes the responsibility of the host to tell the guest about the status of the seating. Eye contact should be made with the guests, so that they do not get the impression that the host is trying to brush them off.

Coldness: Have you even been to a restaurant where the food was excellent and the prices reasonable, but you still felt something was missing? That something was a problem that you could not identify. Most of the time, it was that the restaurant left you with a cold feeling toward it. The host who responds to the guest's question with one-phrase or one-word answers is guilty of committing the sin of coldness.

For example, a guest might ask the host, "How long has the restaurant been in business?" The host answers,

"Two years." The next question is also answered with a brisk reply. This is the one opportunity for the host to make the guest the restaurant's ally; instead, the host has turned off the guest. Answers are best if they are complete and friendly. This will benefit the restaurant in two ways. First, the guest will have questions answered, and second, it will create a warm feeling toward the restaurant by the guest.

Condescension: Condescension can be described as an air of superiority that an individual shows toward another person. A host who is guilty of the sin of condescension would give the guest the impression that he or she does not belong in the restaurant. Unfortunately, condescension is, frequently directed at high school students. This most often occurs when they have a prom, and go to the dinner before the dance. The host's attitude conveys the impression to the staff that the high school students are not very good customers. Notice the word customers is used, not guests, That is an example of a condescending attitude. To correct this problem, the host should lead by setting an example, and should treat all the individuals who enter the restaurant as guests.

All guests receiving positive treatment by all employees will increase repeat business for the establishment. The host or the staff should not be allowed to feel that they are better than any of the guests. By treating the high school student as guests, and by realising that this is an important night for them, the host can make them feel important. Therefore, the host should greet them warmly and treat them like the valued, respectable guests they are.

Robotism: Robots do not belong in the dining room of a restaurant. A robot can do many repetitive, boring tasks well. However, the job of the host is not repetitive or boring. An example of robotism is when the host seats guests. The host picks up the menus; says, "Follow me";

and sprints to the table. The host then places the menus at the place settings and says, "Have a good meal." The next group of people are treated to the same robotic antics. This method of dealing with guests is eventually transferred to the actions of the service staff.

It becomes especially obvious when the service person is going through the "Hi, my name is..." canned speech. To alleviate the sin of robotism, the host should act natural, and should encourage the staff to act natural also. The host's movements should be energetic, and his or her speech should be cordial toward the guests. A robot would be great to do the dishes, but not to manage the dining room.

Rule book excuses: Rules are a necessary part of any business. However, when a host manages only by rules, and does not use common sense, the restaurant will suffer.

A couple decided to try a new restaurant that had windows overlooking beautiful view. The tables directly in front of the windows were all booths for four people. When the hostess seated them at a deuce away from the windows, they asked for a window seat. The hostess said "I'm sorry but I have to save those seats for parties of four." They tried to buy the table by giving her a five-dollar bill. She still said that she could not give them the table. The time was 5 P.m., just when the restaurant opened and there were no other guests demanding to be seated. They could not understand why they could not have the table they desired. During their meal, they watched the table to see how many people she sat at the booths. When they left an hour and a half later, there still were no guests seated at the table they wanted. Of course, they never returned to the restaurant-and apparently not too many others did either, because the restaurant went out of business. This was another example of a host failing at the moment of truth. The host must not fall victim of the sin of rule book excuses, and may bend the rules when it benefits the guests.

The runaround: The final sin of service has been experienced by everyone at one time or another in life- the runaround. An example of this as it relates to the host often occurs when the guest is waiting for a table at a no-reservation restaurant. When the guest approaches the host and asks how long it will be before the party is seated, the host replies, "Just a short time." The guest waits for a table to be vacant, and after twenty minutes returns to the host and asks the same question. Again the host says it will be just a short while. When the guest demands a specific time, the host pretends to check the dining room and gets sidetracked.

The definition of the runaround is to give vague answers or to refuse to answer the question by ignoring or changing the meaning of the question. The way to avoid the runaround is for the host to give definite answers. A definite time will satisfy the guest's question of "How long will it be before the table is ready?" An appropriate answer would be fifteen to twenty minutes, not "In a short while."

Knowing and training the staff to recognise and avoid the seven deadly sins of service is important for the host. The restaurant business is filled with many moments of truth. The restaurant cannot afford to have sins committed at any moment of truth. The first moment of truth comes when the host greets guests into the restaurant. The last moment occurs when the guest leaves the establishment. Throughout their meal, they will experience a series of moments of truth. All of these moments of truth add up to the total service in the restaurant. If the staff fail in one of these moments of truths, then service will suffer.

Warm Greeting

The host is exactly that: a host. The greeting should be

warm and cordial, just as it would be in the host's home. The first thirty seconds are critical for the guest. In those few seconds, the guest forms an opinion about the restaurant: it wants or does not want the guest's business. This is all determined from the greeting offered by the host. The size and volume of the restaurant determine the number of hosts on duty and their responsibilities.

Smaller restaurants usually have one host who has to perform all the jobs. At larger establishments there may be as many as four hosts. One remains at the podium to greet guests, take names, and assign tables. Another finds the guests in the waiting area or at the bar. The other two show the guests to their tables, each being responsible for one half of the dining room. Other establishments use three hosts. One remains at the podium to greet guests, take names, and assign tables. Another gets the guests when their table is ready. The third seats people and does table checks.

Regardless of the size of the establishment or the number of hosts employed, one host is always responsible for greeting the guests. This individual is always in a position to see when a guest enters the restaurant.

Once the guest enters the restaurant, it becomes the host's responsibility to greet the guests immediately. If the host recognises the guests, he or she will greet them by addressing them by name. If the guests are new to the restaurant, the greeting is cordial. When at the podium receiving guests, the host should not be leaning over the desk, chewing gum, smoking, or drinking. Instead, the guests receive the undivided attention of the host. If the restaurant takes reservations, the first question after the greeting will be, "Do you have a reservation?" If the guests do have a reservation, the host takes them to their table. If the restaurant does not take reservations, or the guests do not have a reservation, an inquiry will be made about the size of the party.

CORRECT WAY TO ASSIGN TABLES

As with everything else in the restaurant business, there is a correct way to assign tables. There are also those hosts who take shortcuts and create problems for the guests, service staff, and the restaurant. Assigning tables correctly is another step to ensure that the restaurant obtains maximum income and the guests receive excellent service.

A good tactic used by many restaurants is to seat the guests who arrive when the restaurant opens at a table by the window. Studies have shown that people would rather dine in a busy restaurant than one that is not busy. If the host seats guests near a window, people walking or driving by will see the guests enjoying a meal, and it will create an impression in their minds that the restaurant is a good place to dine.

Rotation of the seating of the guests among the different stations is also advised. The wrong way to seat guests is for the host to seat the first twenty guests at one station, and then fill up the next section. Instead, the first party is seated at station one, the second at station two, and so on. Rotating the seating in this manner allows the service person to give the guests excellent service. If the service person's station were filled up all at once, the service person would have difficulty giving the guests good service because he or she would be overwhelmed with too many guests to serve at once. The rotation of assigning tables is also considered when stations are made and reservations are being blocked.

Occasionally a guest will request a special table or a different table from the one the host assigns. If the host can honour the request, it is good policy to do it. If there is a legitimate reason not to honour the request, it should be explained to the guest. For example, many times guests will request a 4-top for their party of two. If there is not too much business forecasted for the day, the host can give them the table they desire.

If the host expects a heavy demand of business or has a reservation for the table they desire, the guests should be told the reason why they cannot have the table. Of course, if they are regular guests, the host should try to accommodate them and provide them the table. Always seat parties of two at 4-tops if those tables are not in demand.

When a large group of people request a table together, the host should inquire whether they are on a time schedule (sometimes guests are attending a conference and have only a limited time to eat). If they are, it would be wise for the host to explain that it would be faster service if the party broke up into groups of four. The host could then seat the guests at different stations in the dining room. In this way, they will have more service staff to wait on them, instead of just one service person.

Need Forms

In addition to the ability to think quickly, the host needs a few forms that will assist in doing the job correctly and efficiently. The forms needed are: a diagram of the tables in the restaurant, the reservation list, the turnsheet, a table check form, and a waitlist.

Diagram of the Tables

At the host's desk, there should be a diagram of the floor plan of the restaurant. Many restaurants place this diagram under a glass top. The hosts are given a grease pencil so they can write on the glass to indicate the vacant or occupied status of the table. Using the grease pencil and glass top makes it easier for the host to keep track of the status of the tables. It is also easier to erase and neater than trying to keep track on individual paper diagrams.

List of Reservations

Along with the diagram of the restaurant, the host should also have an alphabetised list of the names of the guests who have reserved a table. Included on the list should be the names of the guests, the number of guests, and the table number they have been assigned. The list should be set up in chronological order. This will allow the host to check off the names as the guests come in to the restaurant, and will make for a smoother operation.

The listing would continue throughout the entire day. By setting this up in an organised fashion, the host can spend time attending to the guests' needs. If the host did not write this seating out in advance, he or she would have to spend an enormous amount of time and effort correctly seating the guests with reservations.

The Turnsheet

The next form needed to seat guests effectively is called a turnsheet. The turnsheet shows that have five service staff. After each person's name there is a series of numbers. The top number of the fraction represents the number of guests in the party.

Most hosts use the turnsheet to seat the guests equitably among the service staff. However, when the restaurant becomes busy, often the host has no choice but to seat the guests at the next available table. However, in order to avoid a controversy with the service staff, it is advisable for the host to keep track of the guests served by using the turnsheet.

Restaurants that do not take reservations, or only reserve a small percentage of tables, need a method to seat the guests. When there are tables available, there are no problems; guests are seated at an available table. Problems arise when all tables are occupied. No guest wants to be treated in the following manner. In this no-reservations policy restaurant, when guests approached the host and asked for a table, the host would seat them.

However, if the dining room was full, the host would tell the guest to go to the bar and check back in a few moments. The guest would say, "Aren't you going to put my name down?" The host would reply, "No." The guest wanted to know how he would know when his table would be ready. `Just come back, and if there is a table you get it," said the host. The guest suggested that a better method would be to take his name down. The host replied, "What do you think I am, a secretary?" The host is no longer employed at this establishment.

Table Check

The table check is a tool that allows the host to know the point of the meal that each table has reached. This form is continuously updated throughout the meal. For instance, some restaurants will have it done every twenty minutes. The table check is completed by one of the hosts whose job it is to walk around the dining room and observe each table's progress. The host writes down the

Some restaurants do table checks every twenty minutes, while other hosts do table checks informally. The host remains at the desk greeting guests, while another employee roams throughout the dining room, communicating the -availability of the tables directly to the host via a headset microphone. Once the host knows how long the wait will be, the proper method of informing the guest of the wait for the table can be used.

Waiting Time

When a guest arrives at a restaurant that does not take reservations and there is a long waiting time, the host has an obligation to tell the guests approximately how long they will have to wait for a table. Most guests do not mind waiting; however, some guests will object. The host should never state to a guest that it will just be a few minutes for a table. Instead, the host should give the guest an approximate time. This time has to be one that the host can honour. For example, if the host knows that a table will be vacant in fifteen minutes, the guest should be told that there is a wait of fifteen to twenty minutes. If the guest is seated before the fifteen minutes, that will be great for the guest. If the wait is more than twenty minutes, the restaurant has failed in this moment of truth.

When the host informs the guest of the length of the wait, the responsibility of staying or leaving rests upon the guest. Many restaurants have a friendly working relationship with their competitors. The host will phone the competitors and find out how long a wait there is at the competitor's restaurant, if any. The host can use this information in a variety of ways to assist the guests. First, if there is a long wait at the competitor's restaurant, this knowledge relayed to the guests may keep them at the host's restaurant. This is especially true after the guests have to factor in driving time to the competitor's restaurant. However, if the competitor has space available or a much shorter waiting list, this can be relayed to the guests.

The host should keep the guests informed whenever possible about problems that arise that may keep the table from being available when promised. If guests cannot be seated when promised, management policy may allow the host to give the guests some complimentary item to let them know that their business is appreciated. One restaurant takes this a step further. Any guests who are told the waiting time and decide that it is too long for them to stay, receive a card that can be redeemed for a complimentary drink on their next visit to the restaurant.

Waitlist

All restaurants that take walkins must have a waitlist. This form allows the host to seat guests in an organised manner. The waitlist is used when all the tables are occupied in the restaurant and guests are waiting for a table. The waitlist is set up with the names of the guests who are waiting for a table. The next column is for guests who want a table for four or more guests. The number in parenthesis, 51, represents the table that the host plans to use for that party. Est. wait time refers to the amount of time the host has estimated that the guest will have to wait for a table. Time in refers to when the guest entered the restaurant. Time seated is when the guest has been seated at the table. The next column is for groups of two. Finally, the table number where the guest was actually seated is recorded.

Table are Ready: Informing Guests

Different establishments have different methods for informing their guests when their tables are ready. Many have loudspeakers that announce their names. A more professional method is to have a system that instructs the bartenders and cocktail servers to ask the guests if they are having dinner. If the guests say they are, they ask them for their card. When their table is ready, the host calls the bar and informs the bartender that there is a table available for the Smith party of two. Another method is for the host to walk through the waiting area and announce the names of the guests that he or she is seeking.

At a twentieth-year high school reunion, a classmate boasted that he had never waited very long for a table at places that had a no-reservation policy. He and his date would go to restaurants that took the names of walk-in guests waiting for a table. Sometimes, they would go to the bar and have a drink; other times they would obtain their table immediately. This is how he did it: As soon as he heard the host calling the name and number of guests in the party, (for instance, the Smith party of two), he would go to the host and claim the table. Most of the time he was seated because the restaurant did not give out any cards to the guests.

Another method uses technology. Guests waiting for a table are given pagers and allowed to roam the vicinity. When their table is ready, they are beeped by the host. Of course, a few pagers may be lost by forgetful patrons.

Accurate waitlist

The host must keep an accurate waitlist to avoid problems in seating guests, and to aid in planning future business. All restaurants have their own codes to assist them with the waitlist. At one restaurant, when a guest requests a table for six, the host places a big black mark around the guest's name. This is to signify that they have a large party waiting. As the number of tables that will accommodate six people are limited, the host does not want to make the guest's party wait longer than they are told.

In addition, once the host sends for a party, he or she underlines the name with the black pen. When the person has been located, the host puts a double mark under the name. If a person is not found, he or she puts down the time the guest was called, gives them fifteen minutes to appear, and if they are not there in that time, puts in large letters NS (for No-Show) through their name. The information gained from the waitlist can be valuable for the host. The host can see how many guests had to wait for a table, the time the first guest had to wait, the average waiting time, the longest waiting time, and other factors that will help the host staff and plan for the business.

Once the host reaches the table, it is proper to pull out chairs for the guests (women first) and assist them with seating. If the table is against the wall, it has become traditional to offer the seat that faces into the dining room to the female, while the male is seated facing the wall. The napkins are removed from the table by the host, opened, and handed to the guests.

Menus should be distributed next, both food and wine, if appropriate. Women are given their menus first. It is advisable to open up the menus to the entree page. This accomplishes two things. First, the host can see if the menu is the correct menu; second, it is another small detail that the guest will not have to attend to. Next, the host has to communicate important information to the guests.

Information Communication

This is an area where most hosts fall short. Many hosts bring the guest to the table, drop off the menus, and are never seen again. After the guests have been seated and handed menus, the host should inform the guests of any chef's creations (and their prices) that are not listed on the written menu. The restaurant should not have more than three chef's specials, because the guests may become confused. Many restaurants use an alternative method. The host gives a list of daily specials to the guests along with the regular menus. The host points out the list, which includes prices, to the guests as they are seated.

It is strongly suggested that the host use the guests' names as much as possible when they are known. Once the guests have been told the additions to the menu, the host may also ask them if they would like to order a beverage. This is a key moment of truth in the restaurant business.

By having the host take the drink order, the guest will have been served immediately. The restaurant is saying to the guest that we value your business and do not want you to wait for anything. In addition, there is the possibility of selling more drinks, whether they are alcoholic or nonalcoholic. This serving or taking of a drink order should be done with every meal period. At breakfast, the host would offer coffee to the guest immediately. The last thing the host should do as he leaves the table is to tell the guests the name of the service person. To be most effective, it should be done in an informal manner, such as, "Jan will be your service person, she will be right over with your drink order." As the host leaves the table, the drink order is given to the service person so it can be delivered as soon as possible. The host can now concentrate on working the floor.

WORKING THE FLOOR

Working the floor is a phrase used in the restaurant business to mean that the host is circulating around the dining room talking to guests and assisting service staff. When the guest has been seated by the host, the host should not go back and stand at the podium waiting for the next guest to come into the restaurant. Instead, the host has to walk around the dining room and make certain that the guests are being served properly. One of the key factors in working the floor is to communicate with the guests. If the host notices that the guests are sitting at the table with their menus for a long period of time, he should approach the table and ask, "Has Jan been here to take your order yet?"

Working the floor also involves "getting your hands dirty." This means that the host (and dining room manager, if they are not the same . person) may bus tables, serve food, serve drinks, and reset tables if a service person needs assistance. The host should be not just a pretty face but a vital working member of the staff. The final responsibility of the host is to make sure that the guests are completely satisfied with their dining experience. As the guests complete their meals, the host inquires about their dining experience and shows appreciation to the guests for patronising the restaurant.

This appreciation can be shown in the form of a "Thank you," buying the guest a free dessert or after-dinner drink, or some other gesture that makes the guests feel special. Other establishments empower the host and the waitstaff to give a card to their guests that offers them a free appetizer or dessert upon their next visit.

A couple were at a restaurant. They watched and listened as the host approached and spoke to a party of two after they had finished their meal. One guest had ordered swordfish that was served on a bed of pasta. The host inquired about the food, asking how they liked it. The guest said that the swordfish was great, but the pasta was not cooked enough. The host replied that all the pasta is cooked the same way, al dente. He further added: "If you want, you can take the pasta home with you and microwave it. It will taste really good that way. The next time you come in, make sure you ask for it (the pasta) cooked more than al dente." If you were the guest would you be pleased with this response? What do you think the host did correctly and incorrectly? What improvements could you suggest to make the guest feel satisfied?

Guests with Disabilities

There are specific guidelines for both new and existing

restaurants that must be followed. The dining room manager should be aware of this law and the guidelines that must be followed. If the restaurant is not accessible, a plan should to put into effect to make the restaurant accessible. As an example, it has been reported that Planet Hollywood in Washington, D.C., has agreed to install a ramp leading to the front entrance, place an accessible restroom on the first floor, lower counters in the bar and retail areas, build a ramp into the science fiction theme dining area and install signage required by the ADA. This occurred because of a complaint brought by wheelchair users Atsuko Kuwana and her husband, Michael Winter, after they had to enter through a locked side service door because the three steps leading to the front entrance allegedly were not ramped.

With restaurants becoming more accessible to guests with disabilities, the host has to be aware of what can be done to make their dining experience enjoyable. The type of disability guests have will dictate their special needs as well as the consideration that the host gives them. For instance, a visually impaired guest should be led to the table and have the location of the utensils explained by the host by imagining the table as the face of a clock (e.g., the coffee cup is at five o'clock). If the guest has a seeing-eye dog, the host leads the guest to a table where the dog can lie down without being in the traffic flow.

In addition, guests must be seated in the least restrictive environment. A host cannot give people with disabilities the poorest table in the restaurant. The host would seat guests in wheel-chairs at a table that is out of the flow of traffic, but where the guest is comfortable.' The host may assist the guest in whatever way possible to make the person feel welcome. It may be necessary to move the table so the guest can position his or her wheelchair comfortably at the place setting. In some instances, it might be necessary to raise the table to a height that will accommodate wheelchairs.

Regardless of the disability of the guest, the host has to remember, and impress upon the staff, that these individuals are as valuable to the restaurant as guests who are not disabled. The staff has to be taught to treat all guests with courtesy, and to put forth extra effort so that all can enjoy themselves and have a pleasant dining experience.

Unfortunately, there will be times when a guest has a complaint about the wait for the table, the food, the services, or prices. The host must know how to handle complaints and be able to resolve the situation so the guest feels that the problem has been solved satisfactorily.

Handling Complaints

1. Give undivided attention and listen carefully to the guest's complaint.
2. Clarify the complaint by repeating it back to the guest.
3. Agree with the guest on some point about the complaint.
4. Solve the guest's problem. Ask what he or she would like you to do, or explain why the complaint cannot be solved.
5. Check back throughout the meal to be certain the problem was solved.

Clarify the complaint by repeating it back to the guest. By now the guest should have calmed down. Make the person realise that you understand the complaint. Next, try to agree on some point about their complaint. Finally, solve the problem or offer the guest some possible solutions to the problem. Throughout the meal, return to the guest's table and check to ensure that the problem has been solved. Using this approach, the host can turn a bad situation into a good situation. This skill in handing complaints is another area that the host must excel in to create a positive moment of truth for the restaurant.

Problem of Not Honouring Reservations

Unfortunately, one of the major problems that occurs in restaurants is that reservations are not honoured. This happens for a number of reasons. Occasionally there will be a problem because reservations have been taken incorrectly. Other times, guests will stay longer than their residence time. Regardless of the problem or reason why the restaurant does not have a table for the guests, it is the fault of the restaurant, not the guests.

To solve the problem, the host must seat the guests as soon as a table becomes available. However, the host first should explain the problem to the guests and offer an apology for their inconvenience. It is recommended that the host make some positive gesture to the guests to soothe their feelings for their inconvenience. If it is legal in your state, buy them a bottle of wine with the meal; or have them go to the bar and buy them a drink. If they don't drink, offer them a free dessert.

In the meantime, the host also has to deal with guests who are staying past their residence time. The host should find out the reason for the delay. If it is a problem that can be solved quickly (the service person has not given the guests their check), the host can rectify it immediately. The table can now be set (called turning tables) for the next guest. If the guests are sitting with an extra cup of coffee, the host may not be able to do anything. Or an offer may be made to move the guests to another area (such as the bar or a sitting room), where they can continue their conversation. However, this is a very tricky situation, and the host may do more harm than good by asking the guests to move. This is a decision that the host would make after considering whether asking the guests to move would create negative feelings in the guests.

After the problems have been solved, the host must identify the reason why the reservations were not honoured. Then, adjustments to the reservation policy must be made so the problem will not occur again. The host must be able to solve the problem of not honouring reservations, so the guest will want to return to the restaurant for another meal.

The host's job is not complete until long after the guests leave the restaurant. After the guests have received their entrees, the host works the floor and talks to the guests, inquiring about their meals. Before the guests leave the restaurant, the host should inquire about the dining experience and offer the guests something free. This could be an after-dinner drink, dessert, or complimentary coffee. The key is to let the guests know that their business is appreciated.

Logbook

Each restaurant should have a book that includes a record of the important happenings of the day. Items such as the number of meals hat were served, the waiting time of reservations, the time first seated, and other items that will assist in the forecasting of the business may be included in the logbook. In addition, there is usually an area where messages are left for the next shift. By having this special area in the logbook, no messages are lost and there is proof that information was passed to the next shift. This logbook will help the restaurant run smoothly and efficiently.

Marketing Plan

All businesses, regardless of type, need a marketing plan.

The plan is a blueprint for the business. Because the only constant in the business world is change, the restaurant or banquet manager has to complete this blueprint to guide the business for the upcoming year. A marketing plan lets management know where the business is at present. It outlines problems and opportunities by identifying the operation's strengths and weaknesses as well as its competitors. Goals are set and strategies are planned based upon an analysis of the strengths and weaknesses. The marketing document will state how the plan will be implemented and executed. Included will be a budget to help the operation reach its desired goals. Finally, the plan will have criteria built into it to allow management to determine if the plan has been successful.

8

PREPARATION OF BANQUET EVENTS

Now the banquet manager's most critical part of the job begins. The banquet manager must plan and organise the minute details of the function to make it a success. The banquet manager takes the responsibility for the event off of the client's shoulders and puts it on his or her own shoulders. Great service will be made up of many moments of truth that the banquet manager must control. If the banquet manager successfully attends to the details of planning, organising, and managing the function, the event will be successful.

The banquet manager must use the information on the function sheet to organise, plan, and manage the wedding. The function sheet has been distributed to the department heads. Using the function sheet, the department heads have scheduled employees and obtained the food and beverages needed for the event. The banquet manager will make any last minute changes on the function sheet and forward them to all the department heads, highlighting the changes. These were obtained when the guarantee was obtained from the client.

The first job the banquet manager has to perform after the guarantee is received is to make certain there are the proper number of employees to serve the party. The banquet manager should be concerned with the number needed not only of service staff, but also of the bar and kitchen staff. The banquet manager is the one ultimately responsible for the service of the banquet. Having too few bartenders or kitchen staff results in slow service for the guests.

Service Staff

The amount of staff that is scheduled by banquet establishments varies depending upon the number of guests at a table, the competency of the staff, and whether the staff is covered by union representation (in the case of union representation, the amount of staff required is clearly stated in the contract). Generally, one service person can serve between sixteen and twenty-four guests efficiently. Using this figure, one service person should be scheduled to serve two or three tables, depending on how many guests are seated at each table. For a buffet or cocktail party with butler service, one service person is needed for thirty-five guests. At a cocktail party, without butler service, one server is needed for every fifty guests.

At the wedding, ten service personnel should be scheduled. Each person will serve approximately twenty guests. Because the cocktail party is before the main meal, some of the same staff can be used to pass the food butler-style during the cocktail reception.

Bar Staff

Normally, at a cocktail reception, either before dinner or by itself, one bartender is needed for every fifty guests; after dinner, one is needed for one hundred. This applies to both cash and open bars. Often extra bartenders are needed only for the cocktail reception. As they are only needed for a short period, it becomes expensive to employ them for the entire night or for the minimum required by some state laws. One way to alleviate this problem is to have service people act as bartenders. Another method is to schedule bartenders from a previous party to work one or two hours overtime.

For instance, if a bartender is scheduled to work from 10 A.m. to 6 P.m., have the bartender stay for two hours of overtime. During that period from 6 P.m. to-8 P.m., the bar-, tender can set up the bar and serve the guests at the cocktail party. When the cocktail party is finished, the bartender is done working.

Kitchen Staff

The staffing of the kitchen is an area of the function to which most banquet managers do not give proper consideration. At a banquet it is extremely important to serve the food as quickly as possible from the kitchen to the guests. In order to do this, the kitchen must be organised. If this has been delegated to a proven knowledgeable chef, your worries are over. If you have not worked with each other, you ought to work together to get the food plated efficiently and quickly.

There are two methods for serving that work well. Both methods need teamwork to serve the meal quickly. Only one skilled culinary person is required to be at each serving line. The other employees put the food on the plate and have to be able to work quickly. Both systems work fastest when the meat has been sauced before being placed on the plate.

The first method, which was used at Hotel, is shown in Figure 1. This requires four people at each station to serve the food. Each person has a specific item to put on the plate. There are two piles of plates. Employee 2, the skilled employee, puts on the main course, while employees 3 and 4 put on the potato and vegetable. Very quickly, they develop a rhythm to avoid crashes. The plate never moves until employee 1 removes it and puts the sauce on the meat, if needed. The service person garnishes the plate, covers it, and takes it out of the kitchen.

The other method, just as effective, is shown in Figure 2. This method, used at the Hall of Springs in Saratoga, New York, is similar to the DeWitt Clinton method. Three piles of plates are set up on a rectangular table. Employee 1 puts the main course item on plates from any one of the three piles. Employees 2 and 3 put on the potato and vegetable.

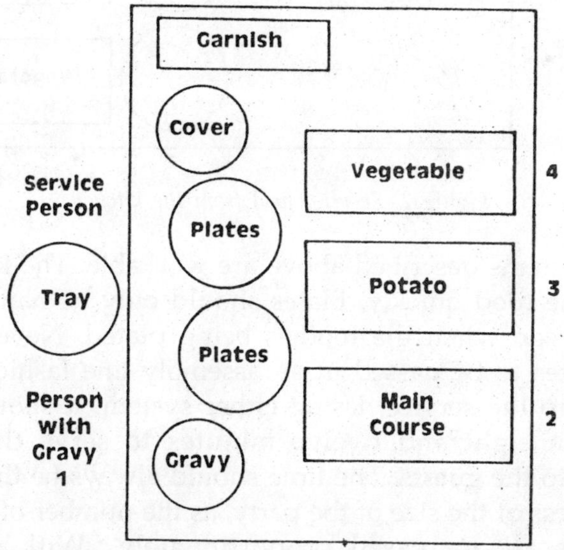

Figure 1. Serving food from the kitchen at a banquet

Both employees (2 with the left hand, 3 with the right hand) pull the plates from the pile when the dish is complete. They place them on the table, and a service person garnishes the plates, covers them, and brings them out into the dining room. A few days before the wedding the banquet manager confers with the chef to develop a plan to serve the function. In a non-union establishment, the extra bartenders, service people, or even dishwashers may help with the planning of the meal.

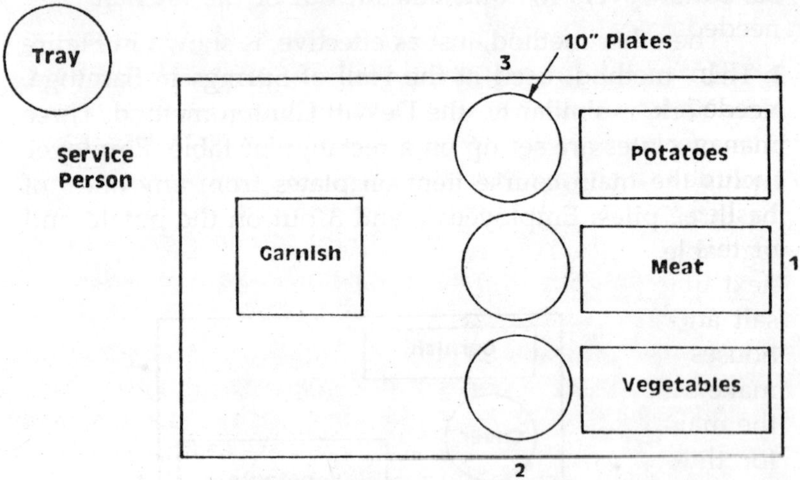

Figure 2. Serving food from the kitchen

Both systems described above are workable. The key is to plate the food quickly. Plates should only be handled by one person when the food is being plated. Never allow the plates to be passed in an assembly line fashion. That slows up the service. Using either system, it should take between eight and twelve minutes to serve the main course to the guests. The time should always be the same, regardless of the size of the party, as the number of serving stations are increased proportionately. With staffing planned, the banquet manager can now finalise the equipment that is needed for the event.

Equipment Planning

Information required for the planning of equipment that is needed for the function is obtained directly from the function sheet. The banquet manager determines exactly what plates and utensils are needed to consume the meal. Using the wedding functions sheet, the banquet manager can plan the equipment that will be needed. It is best to list the menu item along with the equipment that will be needed to eat the item.

In addition to figuring out how much equipment is needed for the guests, there are other items the banquet manager must make sure are available for the event. These include salt and pepper shakers, butter dishes, sugars, roll baskets, and cream containers. Having the correct amount of this equipment adds to the success of the event. The next time you attend a banquet, notice how many sets of salt and pepper shakers are on the tables. Most banquet houses provide one for a table of eight guests. Doesn't it make sense to have one set for every two people? When the main course is served, the guests do not have to wait for the salt and pepper to be used by the other seven people at the table. While they are waiting to use the shakers, their food gets cold. Remember, it is the job of the banquet house to make the guest have a pleasurable experience. Catering to that experience is having everything run so well that the guests never have to ask for any item.

The guests should leave feeling great about the event, but without noticing how the banquet establishment accomplished it. The same provisions should be made for the other items. All the items should be placed within easy reach of the guests. Try it yourself. Sit at a table like the one your guest will sit at and try to reach the items. This little experiment will give you a good idea of what your guests have to go through to obtain these items.

There should be one sugar and creamer for every four people. The rolls should be served hot, in a bread basket. The banquet manager should plan on having one and a half rolls for each guest. In addition, the banquet manager has to order extra napkins for use as sidetowels and for use in the center of the banquet table. These napkins are usually a contrasting colour from the tablecloth, but the same colour as the guest napkins. On the napkin will be placed the ashtrays, rolls, salt and pepper shakers, and other items that the guest needs to enjoy the meal. Another item that has to be ordered is extra bread and butter plates to be used as coffee shields.

Once all this equipment has been calculated, the banquet checklist will be completed. The equipment can be obtained before the service staff arrives by a dishwasher or banquet steward. It should be ready for the service staff to set up the tables when they arrive. Obviously, if some equipment is not available, the banquet manager will know before the party is ready to be set up and can make adjustments.

Tip for Planning for Equipment

Many times it becomes impractical to have all the plates and utensils that are needed to serve the party. The banquet establishment simply may not have a sufficient inventory to have three forks for each guest. If a caterer is renting the equipment, the cost may be prohibitive to rent an additional two hundred forks. The banquet manager has a couple of choices. First, the guest can use the same fork for the salad and main course. The service staff are instructed to leave the fork at the place setting when picking up the salad course. This is not proper service, but it is done.

The best method is to determine what items can be washed and used for another course. For example, at the Lockwood wedding, the plate that is used for the pineapple can be washed, dried, and used for the cake course. The guests would have no idea that they are eating off the same plates that contained the pineapple. Can you discover any other multiple uses of equipment?

Jobs for the Service Staff

When the service staff report to work, there should be a detailed work schedule for them. The banquet manager must plan these jobs before the employees report to work. The banquet manger makes a job duty roster. It should be posted in the same location for each banquet. The service staff are usually scheduled to report to work two hours in advance of the function, or at a time determined by the banquet manager. Once the banquet manager masters this system, the amount of time needed to set up the function room is reduced. This is valuable if the establishment is paying the service staff by the hour. For instance, if a service person gets paid $10 per hour, eliminating one hour's work for ten staff members is a savings of $100. Over the course of a year, it would be a great savings.

Place Setting and Cover

The banquet manager also plans the place setting and cover for the banquet. This information is also obtained from the notes the banquet manager made for the equipment that is needed. One setting is set on one table in the banquet room before the staff arrive. It is called the sample setting.

For the wedding, the banquet manager has decided to use a variation of the banquet setting. The dessert spoon and fork are placed above the starter plate. The coffee cup is already in place. All this is done to save time. If this were Russian banquet service, the coffee cup would be brought when the coffee was served. It would not be preset. In American banquet service, however, the coffee cup is preset. The napkin will be folded in the shape of a candle and placed in the red wine glass. Setting up a sample place setting eliminates any questions the service staff may have.

Room Setting Directions

The proper way to set up a banquet room is to set the tables farthest from the kitchen first and work back toward the kitchen. If, for some reason, the tables are not completely set up when the guests arrive, the service staff do not have to carry items through the guests to the tables in the farthest part of the room. They can continue to work their way back toward the kitchen.

Service for Party

Once the banquet manager has the event organised and the service staff are aware of their pre-party assignments, a decision will be made concerning the best method to serve the food to the guests. There are three styles of service used in American banquet service to serve a party. The first is referred to as the station method; the second is the follow-up method; and the third is called the combination method.

Station Method

In this method, each service person is assigned two tables of either eight or ten guests, for a total of between sixteen to twenty people. The service person is solely responsible for the service at those two tables. This system is best used when a large staff of temporary workers are hired to serve a large party. The advantage of this system is that the banquet manager knows who is responsible for service at all the tables.

This system has two main disadvantages. It is the slowest type of American banquet service. Also, guest tables usually will not be served in the proper order. For example, if Pam had tables 1 and 2, she would serve the guests at table 1 their food. Then she must return to the kitchen to obtain the food for table 2. In the meantime, the service person who has table 3 has already served that table. Table 3 is served before table 2, which is shown in Figure 3.

Another potential problem with using the station method is that service people will only set up their own tables. They will not assist in the setting up of the total banquet room. To avoid this problem, the banquet manager must not give out station assignments until the room is set up. Then the service people should be brought to the tables for which they are responsible, so there will be no mix-up concerning which table should be served by whom.

Follow-up Method

This is the most efficient method and quickest service if the staff can master the system. It takes planning, cooperation, and leadership by the banquet manager, the head service people, and the remaining service staff. For the Lockwood wedding, the staff would be broken up into two teams of five. The responsibility of serving the food and removing the dirty dishes in the banquet room would be divided in half, as shown in Figure 4. Each group would have a head service person to supervise its side of the room. Three members of the team would carry the food into the banquet room. The other two (including the head service person) would serve the food to the guests. The head service person would instruct the other service person in the correct order of service. Each team would obtain its food from an assigned plating area in the kitchen.

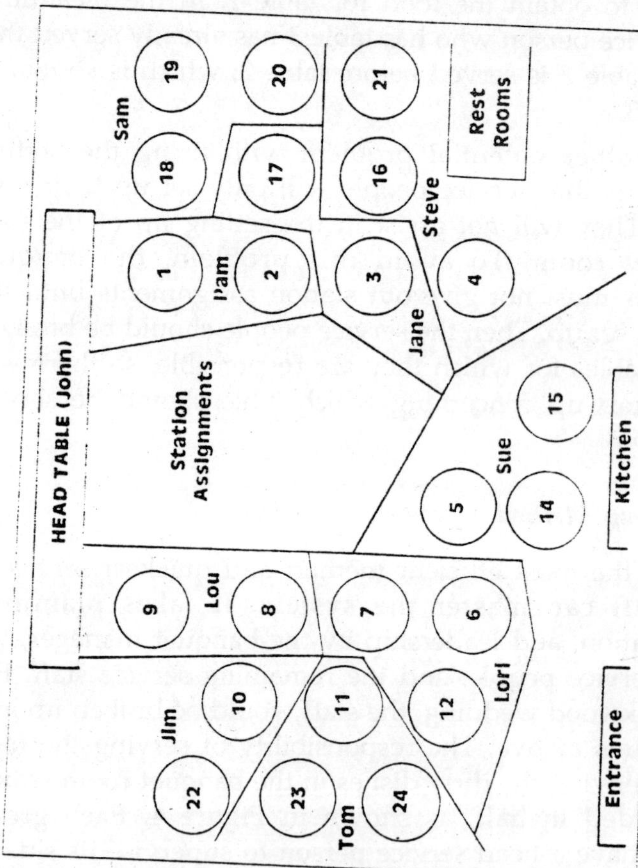

Figure 3. Service stations for an American-style banquet

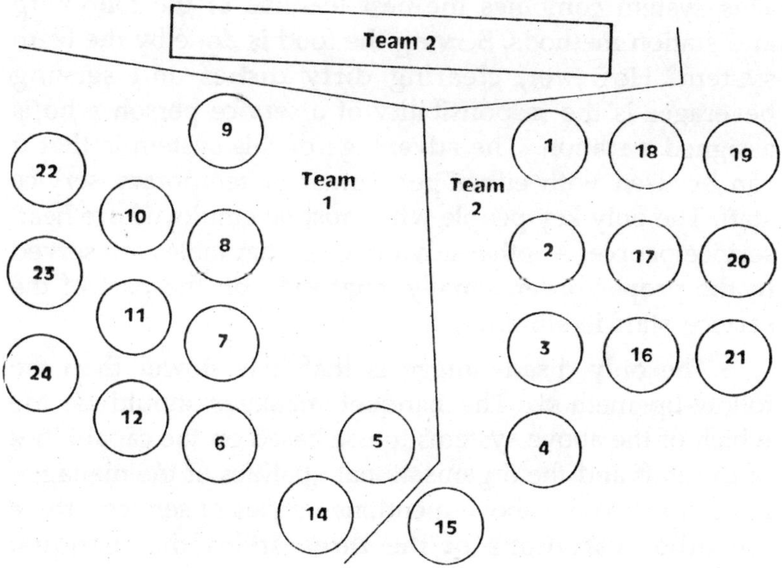

Figure 4. The follow-up method for serving a banquet, the most efficient method and quickest service

When it is time to clear the dirty dishes, all five members of the team work together in removing the dishes. They work from the head table backwards toward the kitchen doors. The banquet manager should be in the banquet room making sure that all the guests get served and that the service is done correctly. The advantages of this type of service are that it is fast and that all the guests are served in proper order. This is considered the best serving system from the kitchen's point of view, because the food is picked up quickly from the kitchen. The main disadvantage is that it is difficult to teach temporary workers to use this system. They generally lack the organisation and team-work it requires.

Combination Method

This system combines the best features of the follow-up and station methods. Serving the food is done by the team system. However, clearing dirty dishes and serving beverages is the responsibility of a service person who is assigned a station. The advantage of this system is that it can be used with either permanent or temporary service staff. The only key people who must be employed are head service people. Another advantage is that tables are served in the proper order. Finally, confusion on the part of the service staff is eliminated.

The only disadvantage is that it is slower than the follow-up method. The banquet manager should decide which of the above systems to use based on the capabilities of the staff and the organisational qualities of the manager. In addition to the above-mentioned styles of services, there are other variations of the three styles that banquet establishments use. For example, a variation of the station method is to have two service staff be responsible for four tables, but have them work as a team. One would carry the food from the kitchen, while the other would serve the food. Regardless of the system the banquet manager decides to use, the main factor in choosing one over the other must be guest satisfaction. Whichever method is used, the banquet manager must be in the dining room at all times when the food is being served and the dirty dishes are being cleared. It is the manager's job to correct mistakes and oversee service.

Proper Order

The banquet manager has to know the correct order in which to serve the guests at a banquet. The head table is always the first table served. Next served are the tables in front of the head table. The service of the rest of the dining room would follow in a logical manner, going from the head table to the back of the room.

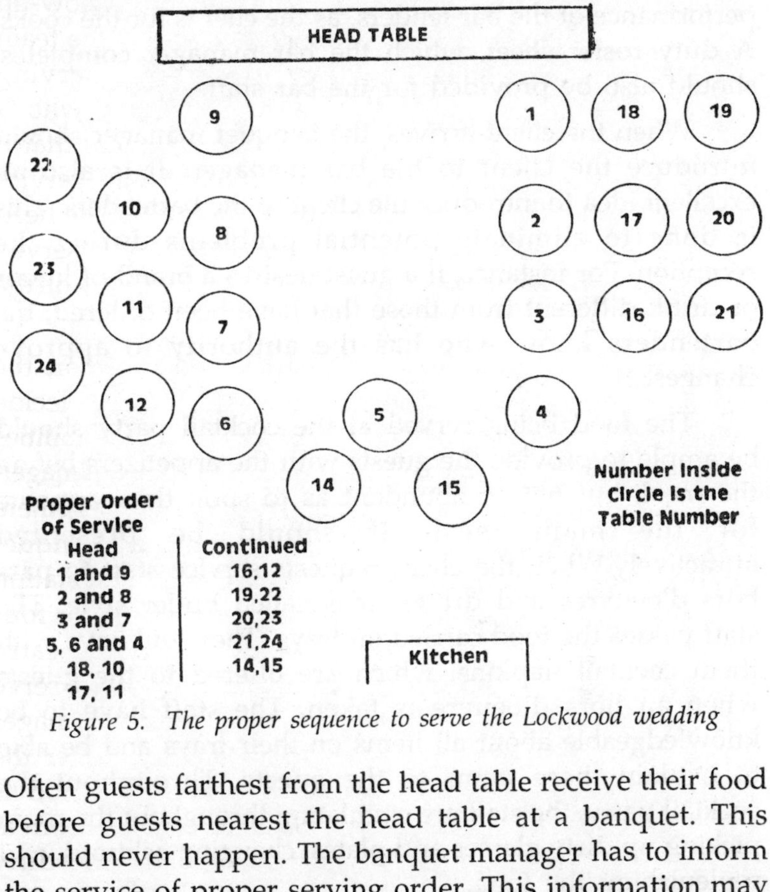

Figure 5. The proper sequence to serve the Lockwood wedding

Often guests farthest from the head table receive their food before guests nearest the head table at a banquet. This should never happen. The banquet manager has to inform the service of proper serving order. This information may be put on the duty roster; however, it works' better when the banquet manager verbally communicates the correct' order to the key staff.

Serving Cocktail Parties

Many times the guest obtains the first impression of service at the banquet establishment during the cocktail reception or party. For this reason, both liquor and food service must be accomplished professionally and with dignity. The bar manager is responsible for the performance of the bar-tenders, as the chef is for the cooks. A duty roster sheet, which the bar manager completes, should also be provided for the bar staff.

When the client arrives, the banquet manager should introduce the client to the bar manager. It is also an excellent idea to introduce the client to the bartenders. This is done to eliminate potential problems during the reception. For instance, if a guest desires a brand of liquor or drink different from those that have been ordered, the bartenders know who has the authority to approve changes.

The food being served at the cocktail party should be ample to provide the guests with the appetizers before the meal, but not so abundant as to spoil their appetite for the main meal. It should be presented attractively.When the client requests service staff to pass hors d'oeuvres and drinks, it is called butler style. The staff passes the food carried on trays. They will have with them cocktail napkins, which are offered to the guests when an hors d'oeuvre is taken. The staff have to be knowledgeable about all items on their trays and be able to explain these items to the guests. Throughout the cocktail party, the staff are circulating throughout the room picking up dirty glasses and plates, changing ashtrays, and replenishing the food.

Tips about Cocktail Parties

Always position bars away from entrances to the room and away from food tables. Plan on staggering the service of hors d'oeuvres. For example, at a cocktail hour, do not serve them all within the first fifteen minutes of the event. Plan to serve the food on small trays staggering the amount of food throughout the cocktail hour. Butler style service, combined with hot and cold food displays, is always the most elegant type of service. This type of service keeps the food looking attractive and stops the guests from crowding around food displays.

The more food that is put out during the cocktail hour, the more food the guests will eat. Guests very seldom will take the last hors d'oeuvre. Instead they will wait until more food is brought out. Therefore, if you have to make food last, don't be too quick to bring out more food. Plan on about five pieces of food per person at a cocktail party before a meal. Supplement the food with a bread and cheese table.

Tip Cups

One repeatedly controversial issue is tip cups for bartenders. Tip cups are placed on the bars to allow the guests to give extra money (to insure prompt service) to the bartenders.

Ending the Cocktail Reception

The banquet manager needs to have a method to end the cocktail party. It must be done without offending the guests or the host. This involves tact and diplomacy. About ten minutes before the cocktail party is scheduled to end, the banquet manager locates the client and informs him or her of the exact time that the cocktail party will end. If a dinner follows the reception, it is critical that the party be ended on time; otherwise the food may be ruined. If no other meal is planned, the client can either end the party or extend it, depending on the policies of the establishment (which were set forth in the policy sheet).

If a meal follows the reception, the banquet manager would then circulate around the room informing the guests that dinner will be served shortly. The guests are asked to proceed to the dining room. Often this information is conveyed by making an announcement via a microphone. Once the host agrees to end the party, the bars have to be shut down quickly. This is a critical moment in a party. The best way of closing bars is to have a prearranged sign with the bartenders. When the sign is given, the bartender should finish serving the drink they are serving, inform the guests that the bar is closed, and walk away from the bar.

RUNNING BANQUET PARTY

When the doors to the banquet room are unlocked to allow guests in, the room has to be completely set to receive guests. All food that is supposed to be present should be in place, and the service staff should be ready to serve the party. The main responsibility of the banquet manager now is to get all the guests seated and the meal served. If the client has arranged seating for the guests, everyone will have a seat and the meal can commence.

However, if there are no seating arrangements, the banquet manager must see that every guest has a seat. This may involve breaking up groups of four or six people and having them sit with guests they do not know. There is a way to avoid having this problem. When the party does not have seating arrangements, select the table that. is the worst location (farthest from the head table, next to the kitchen) and place a reserved sign on it.

That way no guests will sit at that table. The establishment should most likely have the extra table because the banquet establishment usually oversets by 10 percent. Guests coming in early will generally fill up all the other seats. When the latecomers arrive, there is a table left for them. If they don't show up, there is one less table to serve.

Serving and Cleaning

Once all the guests have been seated and the introductions, blessings, or toasts have been given, the service staff can serve the meal. It is the responsibility of the banquet manager to inform the service staff, as well as the kitchen staff, when to serve the meal. No one should serve any food, beverages, or rolls without being told by the banquet manager. The same is true of clearing the dirty dishes. No service person should clean any dirty dishes without authorisation from the banquet manager. The objective in having the banquet manager tell the service staff when to serve and clear is to ensure that all the guests are served approximately at the same time.

Number of Chef

One of the ways the banquet manager ensures a good working relationship with the kitchen is to keep the chef informed about the progress of the party. In order to have a successful banquet, the banquet manager and head service people should count the number of guests that are seated. Once the number of guests has been verified, the banquet manager should give that number to the chef. If there are more or less than the chef planned, adjustments can be made at that time. When late guests arrive, the chef should be informed immediately.

More and more banquet facilities are allowing the client to offer more than one main course choice to the guests attending the event. Some banquet establishments allow as many as three choices. To facilitate the serving of the main course items to the guests, the banquet manger should request that the guests place a colored ticket at their place setting. Each colored ticket represents a particular entree choice. The service people collect the tickets and record which and how many guests are having each item.

When the service people go into the kitchen to pick up the meals, they obtain the correct number of each item for each table. When a follow-up system is used, this requires much more organisation from the staff. Again a reminder: All guests at the table should be served at approximately the same time. A banquet house should not serve all the chicken meals and then serve all the beef meals; but each table should receive the correct number of beef and chicken meals simultaneously.

Proper and Improper Way of Serving

Approximately eighty guests were in attendance. This was a great lesson in how not to serve a banquet. The guests made their choice of what they desired to eat when they RSVPed. However, the service staff did not ask who gets what entree. There were no colored tickets. They simply brought out the main courses. They were short one meal. On the other hand, at a wedding reception for three hundred guests, there were two options: either beef or chicken. The waitstaff asked each guest at each table what they had ordered. They took the orders and served everyone at once.

The difference between the parties: a supervisor was in the room at all times during the wedding reception.

Some clients will only pay their bill based upon the number of meal tickets that are collected. Under these conditions, the banquet manager should have a person in the kitchen collecting tickets from the service people. For example, when the service person picks up ten meals, that person should give ten tickets to the collector. At a buffet, a service person is stationed at the beginning of the buffet line to collect tickets.

The service person should be taught that if a guest does not have a ticket, the banquet manager is to be summoned immediately. The banquet manager then checks with the client of the party to determine if the person is really a guest or a crasher of the party (which happens often at conventions and weddings). As soon as the meal has been served, the banquet manager informs the client of the number of guests that the banquet house has served. If there is a discrepancy, the client and the banquet manager can count the number of guests and solve the problem.

BUFFETS

When the client chooses the option of having a buffet, the banquet manager is responsible for having the buffet set up and ready for the guests at the scheduled time. All buffets have a few basic principles. It goes without saying that all hot food must be served hot and all cold food must be served cold. Buffet lines are arranged so guests will not have to stand in a long line waiting for food. The buffet has to look neat and the food must be appetizing.

Buffets are great for clients who want their guests to have a choice of meal items. Buffets are also great for serving a meal in a room that is located a distance from the kitchen. For instance, using a buffet at a pool is an ideal way to increase the use of the area around the pool, and in turn the revenue of an establishment. Buffets are a lifesaver when the establishment has a limited amount of function rooms. As an example, a group would like to have an all-day meeting with lunch.

The banquet house has only one room that will accommodate the guests. The solution is to have the meeting set up using tables. The client and banquet manager schedule a 30- to 45-minute break before lunch is served. By using a buffet, the establishment can serve the guests lunch. The service persons will not have to set up their utensils and food from the buffet. As with all banquet functions, this service option requires much organisation by the banquet manager to make it a success.

Flow and Layout

If at all possible it is best to have separate islands for the different parts of the meal. There can be a separate table for beverages, one for appetizers and salads, one for main courses, and another for dessert. One buffet line is needed to serve every one hundred guests. The establishment can use ice carvings to keep food cold and chafing dishes or heating units to keep food warm. Food can be displayed on mirrors, in ice carvings, or in edible bread items.

All condiments are to be placed in front of or next to the food they accompany. For example, next to the ham would be mustard. It is recommended that the condiments be placed in monkey dishes (small cup-like dishes), which should have underliners beneath them. The proper utensils to use for the condiments should be placed on the underliner.

Buffet Setting

In the setup of a buffet, the first item at the beginning of the buffet line should be clean plates. The banquet manager instructs the service people to check not only the top of the plates but also the bottoms for cleanliness. The buffet is usually arranged in the same manner as a meal would be served. Appetizers are placed first on the buffet line, followed by salads. Then the main course items, along with the starches and vegetables.

The rolls, butter, utensils, and beverages generally are the last items on the buffet line. Ideally, they should be on a separate table. By placing them at the end of the buffet line, it becomes easier for the guests to select the food and carry their plates without having to balance their

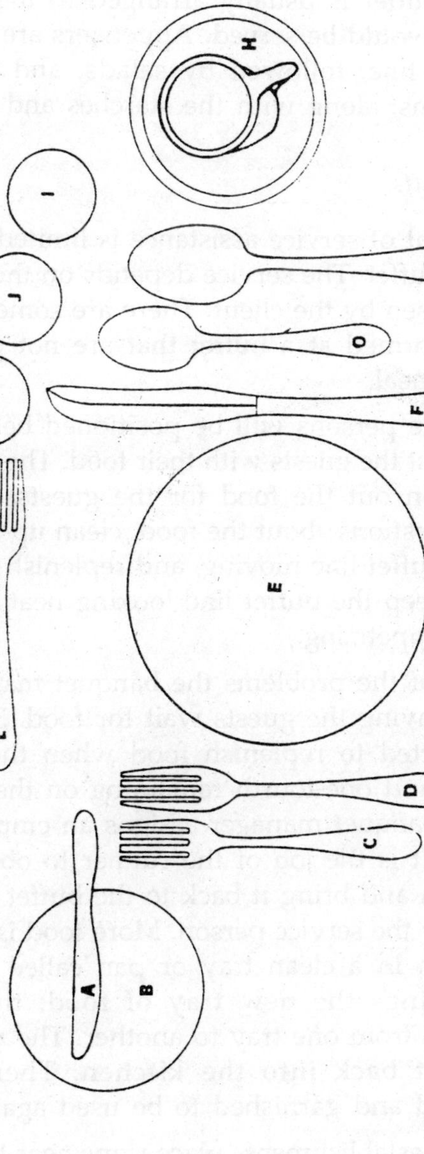

Figure 6. A diagram of the place setting

utensils with their food. Of course, if the banquet establishment wants

The buffet is usually arranged in the same manner as a meal would be served. Appetizers are placed first on the buffet line, followed by salads, and then the main course items, along with the starches and vegetables.

Service Staffs

The amount of service assistance is limited by the service staff at a buffet. The service depends on the style of buffet that is chosen by the client. There are some jobs that have to be performed at a buffet that are not performed at a sit-down meal.

Service persons will be positioned behind the buffet line to assist the guests with their food. The service persons will portion out the food for the guests. They will also answer questions about the food, clean up any food spills, keep the buffet line moving, and replenish the food. Their job is to keep the buffet line looking neat and clean, and the food appetizing.

One of the problems the banquet manager wants to avoid is having the guests wait for food. Service persons are instructed to replenish food when there is between one-third and one-fourth remaining on the tray or in the pan. The banquet manager assigns an employee to act as a runner. It is the job of the runner to obtain food from the kitchen and bring it back to the buffet line when told to do so by the service person. More food is obtained from the kitchen in a clean tray or pan called an insert. The runner brings the new tray of food; the food is not transferred from one tray to another. The remaining food is brought back into the kitchen. There the tray is replenished and garnished to be used again.

Some establishments place signs near the food, which explain the item. This is recommended; however, it is more effective to have knowl-edgeable service staff explaining the food items. If the signs have only the name of the item, the guests may have to ask questions about the food.

Traffc Flow

Another problem that has to be avoided is having all the guests rush up to the buffet table at once to obtain their food. The banquet manager has the responsibility of having the guests proceed to the buffet table in an organised fashion. This is how it is done. When it is time to serve, the banquet manager announces that the guests may proceed to the buffet when their table is called. Informing the guests that they will be called to the buffet alleviates their fears about the establishment running out of food, even if they are the last table to be called. This system allows for a more controlled and civilised manner of serving a buffet.

The first person who has the honor to see and choose the food at the buffet is the client. The banquet manager invites the host's table up to preview the buffet before anyone takes food. After the client's table guests take their food, the banquet manager invites other tables up to obtain their food from the buffet. To keep everyone calm, the banquet manager circulates among the guests telling them when it will be their turn. The next table is invited to proceed to the buffet when there are three or four people waiting in line to obtain their plates. This method eliminates many problems associated with buffets.

If during the preplanning for the event, the client informs you that the buffet must be served quickly, more buffet lines should be set up. Arranging buffet tables so guests may go on both sides of the table works extremely well.

Chafing Dishes

Chafing dishes are used to keep food hot on a buffet. All employees need to know how they work and how to set them up. The chafing dish consists of a frame, two pans, and a top, The top pan fits into the bottom pan, leaving two to three inches of space between the two pans. The bottom pan should be filled with about one inch of hot water.

Underneath the bottom pan, there are one or two containers that hold a can of jellied liquid that will burn for about an hour. This is referred to as canned heat. Sometimes, through careless handling and misuse, the container that holds the canned heat is lost. To solve the problem, an inverted bread and butter dish can be used as a substitute for the container. One problem to avoid is that of placing the canned heat too close to the bottom of the pan. When that occurs the flame from the canned heat will be smothered and it will go out, resulting in cold food. Also, avoid placing the canned heat directly on table surfaces. The can will get very hot and can harm the table.

Approximately ten minutes before the function starts, the service person should light the canned heat. The flame will heat up the water. When the water is heated, the top pan of food may be put into the chafing dish. Cover the food in the pan using the chafing dish top to keep the food hot. The chafing dish will act like a steam table. The heated water creates steam; the top pan does not let the steam out of the chafing dish, and the food stays hot.

During the buffet, the service staff check to make sure that the canned heat does not go out. If it does, it is replaced with another can of heat. The service staff have to be careful to avoid being burned when taking off the covers or replacing a pan of food in the chafing dish.

Tips on Buffet Setting

The buffet should look as appetizing as possible. Many times even though the food is spectacular, the buffet looks boring. This is because the food is not displayed with any imagination.

Platters of food can be raised by using an inverted bread dish. Additionally, height may be created on the buffet table by using crates or boxes covered with linen. Flowers or food items are placed on these covered crates. Dishes with pedestals also add interest and height to a table.

Finally, stand back and look at the buffet. Then make adjustments to the items on the buffet table. These adjustments should be made based on the texture of the dishes, the color of the food, and the position of the items. The banquet manager may position an item away from its normal place to make the buffet more appealing.

Keep Food Hot

Besides using chafing dishes to keep food hot on a buffet, the banquet manager must know how to serve food hot at a sitdown meal. When the banquet manager has to serve a banquet in a room that is adjacent to the kitchen, a detailed plan has to be set up with the chef. In addition, all plates should be heated before the food is placed on them. Some establishments have special heating cabinets, others put the plates in the oven. If the food is placed on a cold plate, it will get cold.

When the banquet is served at a room distant from the kitchen, the food is generally transported in hot carts. Some are electrically heated while others use a form of canned heat to keep the food warm. Again, the key to keeping food hot is to preheat the cart. Once the food arrives at the location, a cook assists in taking the food out of the carts. This cook is responsible for the appearance and quality of the plates. Often, if the menu item requires a sauce, the cook puts it on at this area, which is called the staging area.

Timing is critical in making sure the food is available to be served to the guests when it is scheduled. If the party is to be served at noon, the banquet manager has to plan how long it will take to plate the food in the kitchen, transport it, and serve it, so the guests will obtain their meal at noon.

Serving Sequences

I. The appetizer course is served (from the guest's left side by the service persons left hand). It may be set as a part of the guest's place setting (as was the pineapple).

2. Two roll baskets are served. They are placed in the center of the table by the service person (using the left hand). The rolls should be put in a location that is easy for all the guests to reach. (A small tip: rolls and coffee are a lifesaver when the food is not ready to be served on time. Have the service person serve them to the guests and keep replenishing them. It gives the guests something to eat and drink, but more important it shows them that everything is under control. If the guests were not being served some item, they would be wondering when the food will arrive.)

3. The plate, spoon, and pineapple are removed by the service person (using the right hand, from the guest's right side).

4. The salad is served. At times, the salad can be preset on the table. It should be placed to the left of the salad fork.

5. The salad plate and fork are removed. The champagne glass should also be removed. If the guests have not finished their champagne or salad, instruct the service person to ask if they may be taken away. If the answer is negative, the service person should move the salad out of the center of the place setting and put it to the left of the guest's setting. The service person should also check to see if water glasses and roll baskets need refilling. If they do, the service person should take the roll baskets back to the kitchen and bring them out with the next course. If he or she has time, the service person can refill the water glasses from water pitchers. Ashtrays should be changed, if needed.
6. The main course is served. Meat is positioned in front of the guests so the first cut made by the guest is into the tenderest part of the meal. (Remember: serve all the guests at one table, before serving another table. If the banquet establishment is using a station service setup and the service person cannot carry out ten dinners on the tray, have another service person carry out the remaining dinners so all the guests at the table are served at approximately the same time.)
7. Red wine should be poured by the bartenders. When the service person places a prime rib meal, the bartender should follow by pouring red wine to the guest.
8. The coffee course is served. The service person must use a coffee shield. Tea should be placed in an individual pot above the coffee cup. A wedge of lemon should be served with the tea. At times, the banquet manager can have the service staff put a whole pot of coffee on each table. The guests can pour the beverage themselves. This method is used

especially for breakfast meals or when the client is on a limited time schedule.

9. The main course dishes are removed, along with utensils, red wine glasses, bread and butter plates, salt and pepper shakers, and rolls and butter. The only items left on the table are the utensils for dessert, cream, sugar, water glasses, and ashtrays.
10. Dessert is served, along with more coffee.
11. Dessert dishes, water glasses, utensils, and all items with which the guests have finished are removed. The banquet manager should also have an organised system for putting away items when they are returned to the kitchen. For example, the salt and pepper shakers should always be placed in the same location when they are cleared from the tables.

The banquet manager must be flexible when serving a meal. There are many parts to the meal. Some things may happen that the banquet manager has no control over. The ability to be flexible and to think quickly enough to use whatever items are necessary to keep the guests pleased is critical for the banquet manager.

Latecomers Early-leavers

At many parties, guests will arrive after a few courses have been served. When this occurs, the banquet manager approaches the table and asks the guests if they would like to eat. If the answer is affirmative, the guests are served as quickly as possible whatever courses they desire. It may involve bringing out the pineapple course and salad course together.

You may also encounter guests who must leave in a hurry, before the meal will be served completely. Try to accommodate this type of guest also. This can be done by serving the guest the main course before or while other guests are eating their salad. Both of these types of guests create a problem for the banquet manager. Using tact and diplomacy, the banquet manager can please the client and the guest by accommodating these individuals.

BANQUET CHEEKBAEKS

To be a truly effective banquet manager, it is imperative to check the satisfaction of all the guest tables after the main course has been served to see if the meal and service were satisfactory. An experienced banquet manger will know if the food has been satisfactory by observing the guest's plates. This is the ubiquitous quality needed by the banquet manager. The type of inquiry the banquet manager makes will be determined by the situation that is observed.

For instance, if guests have not eaten their meal, inquire if they would like another choice (if it is possible). A fact to remember is the following: influencing one guest at a banquet has the potential to sell an additional banquet for many guests. It is easier to obtain business from people who have experienced your operation than to create a whole new market. When the opportunity arises that the banquet manager can be introduced to the guests, take advantage of this situation. It will be beneficial for future business.

Throughout the event, the banquet manager should be constantly communicating with the client. The client has to be informed of what will happen next (such as the cake cutting ceremony). The banquet manager continues to inquire whether everything meets the client's satisfaction.

Keep in mind that musicians and photographers love to work at an establishment where the banquet manager informs them of the time and location of events at the function. If the banquet manager makes it easy for these individuals to do their job, it will benefit the establishment, because they will recommend the establishment to potential clients.

Meeting and Business Room

Another type of business that the banquet manager may have concerns meeting rooms. Knowing the correct way to set up the rooms is important, but just as important is knowing how to manage the meeting room business. Coffee breaks are often scheduled in the meeting rooms that the banquet establishment has to set up. As in other types of banquet management, the key to having repeat conference business is to make sure all items are in place and the room is correctly set up for the guests before they arrive.

Items such as water, glasses, pads, pencils, and ashtrays, if they are desired, should be on the tables. One water pitcher should be available for four guests. When the coffee break is scheduled for a specific time, make certain that the coffee and food arrive on time. The timing is critical, but just as important is what happens while the guests are having their coffee break. During the break, the banquet manager should have a member of the staff in the meeting room, replenishing the water, cleaning ashtrays, and freshening up the room for the remainder of the meeting.

Again, organisation is the key to successful meeting room business. All the equipment needed to freshen up the room should be set up outside the room in advance of the coffee break. At break time, the staff simply enter the room and replace, for example, the empty water pitchers with full ones.

Bill Preparation and Rebooking

The banquet manager's last job on the day of the function

should be to present and explain the bill to the client. Payment should be obtained and the client should be thanked for holding the function at the establishment. Finally, if the function is an annual event, ask the client if it may be rebooked for the following year, If the function was a wedding reception, ask the client to recommend your establishment to any future bride and groom.

When it is time for the party to end, inform the client. As the guests and client are leaving the banquet, assist the client with presents, the top of the wedding cake, or any other items with which he or she needs assistance. Once the guests have departed, there is still work to be done. The banquet manager should have a system for cleaning up the dining room.

The dirty dishes and equipment must be brought into the kitchen in an organised fashion. For instance, the staff should go into the dining room with big pots and glass racks. Glasses on the tables should have their contents dumped into the pots. The glasses can then be put into the racks, ready to be washed. Using a system like this eliminates confusion and breakage in the kitchen. Finally, when the banquet room and kitchen are cleaned up to your satisfaction, the employees should be thanked and dismissed. And you, the banquet manager, should feel proud that you have just completed another great function!

The food service industry has been sued increasingly by guests who claim they fell at the restaurant or received chipped teeth or caused their bridgework to fail. These are among the most common complaints that spark threats of legal action against food service establishments.

Running a food service operation leaves a business open to some strange legal cases. Managers should be aware of the types of cases that have been filed and what advice experts have given on how to avoid these lawsuits.

Attorneys and food service professionals indicate that detailed hiring and firing guidelines are a must. Preemployment screening is needed to eliminate potentially violent or otherwise undesirable job candidates. Regularly updated and widely posted written policies against discrimination or harassment of any kind are also recommended. Managers must be aware of and adhere to prevailing wage and hour laws. The maintenance of safe work and public areas is required. Finally, ongoing worker education related to safely preparing and handling food is recommended.

9

ORGANISING EVENTS AND FUNCTIONS

In larger establishments, there may be a catering and sales manager, as well as a group sales office that has the responsibility of booking the function. Once the event is booked, the responsibility for the success of the event belongs to the banquet manager. Conducting stressful functions begins with proper booking of the event. Regardless of the type of function that will be booked, the person booking the function must know specific facts about the individual banquet facility. First, the booking person has to know the number of rooms available and each room's capacity for either meal or meeting functions. Second, the type of physical setups that will accommodate guests comfortably and efficiently in each room should be known. Third, the banquet manager has to know the equipment available to be used in the establishment; whether it has been assigned to another function at the same time, as well as how, where, and at what cost extra equipment can be obtained. Finally, the manager will have to be able to perform the job without having to ask any questions about the room layout.

Architects and banquet managers never see a room the same way. It has been well documented that most restaurant facilities (especially kitchens) are designed by people who do not or have never worked in a kitchen. The same is true of function rooms. Many times, the square footage available is calculated upon the general formula of eight to twelve square feet of space for each person at a sit down meal function. Often, even though the formula is mathematically accepted, the projected number of guests will not fit into the room.

This is because each function is an individual party which may require different demands on the space, resulting in a different capacity for the room. The location of exits, the shape of the head table, the traffic flow, the dance floor, the audio-visual equipment, and the type of function must be taken into consideration before the realistic capacity of a room, for each function, can be determined. For instance, more people will be accommodated in a room when it is being used for a stand up cocktail party rather than for a meeting.

Therefore, the banquet manager should get the "feel of the room" by setting up tables and conducting a few sample functions in it. By doing this, the banquet manager will generally know the capacity of each room for most kinds of functions. Another "moment of truth" occurs when guests sit down to have their meal. If there is enough room at the table, they are pleased. If the room is too crowded, the banquet facility has failed this "moment of truth." Therefore, each person booking functions has to be aware of the realistic capacity and use of every room for every type of function, not relying on the proposed capacity determined by the architect.

Types of Functions

Guests do not want to be too crowded into a room; nor do they want a room where there is so much extra space that it looks as if the party is a failure. It is the banquet manager's responsibility to know the different ways a room can be set up to create a successful social or business event. Banquet managers must know how to use room space effectively in order to maximize revenue. In addition, anyone booking parties has to know the definition of the standard types of functions.

Tables: All guests are seated at tables and are waited on by a service person. For social events, such as weddings or dinners, round tables are ideal because they encourage conversation. For business meetings, a block table, a T-shaped table, or an E-shaped table is better because it eliminates unnecessary conversation. The block table is made up of four rectangular tables put together to form a block. This is an ideal setup for a maximum of twenty guests at a small business meeting where all guests can communicate freely. The T-shaped table is ideal to use in a long, narrow room. The illustration shows three rectangular tables; however, in actual practice, four or five tables would make up the base of the T. The third, the E-shaped table is ideal where there is a large delegation of guests who must be seated at the head table.

Meeting setups: Usually there are two general types of setups for meetings. The easiest one to set up is referred to as theatre style. The guests are provide only chairs, all facing in the same direction. This type of physical setup would be used when the guests are listening to a presentation. The second type of meeting where all the guests have to face the front of the room is set up in a style called schoolroom or classroom. This setup would be used for a teaching seminar. Schoolroom style takes up the most amount of space, which results in a lessening of the amount of guests that may be accommodated in a room.

Head tables: These tables are placed in front of the room, with the guests seated only on the side of the table from which they are facing the other members of the party.

A new trend, at social events, is to have a round head table placed in the middle of the party. This eliminates the formality of the event and allows the guests at the head table to enjoy themselves more.

Cocktail parties: The flow of guests is important for this type of function. The banquet manager can become creative and use all types of space for these parties. It can be the lobbies or pools of hotels, or it can be a function room. The position of both the bars and food stations becomes important for guest comfort and ease of service. Setting up a cocktail party is relatively easy because the banquet manager only has to use a few tables. At a cocktail party, there should be fewer chairs than the number of guests that are expected. This forces the guests to socialise. Care must be used in locating food and drink stations away from one another to minimize traffic jams and facilitate mingling. A popular cocktail party concept that has caught on is to have stations where food is cooked and small portions are served to guests.

For instance, there may be a fettuccine station, a chicken cordon bleu station, and a veal marsala station. More room must be allowed for this type of cocktail party than the traditional one in which food is precooked and put out for the guests in chafing dishes and on trays. At cocktail parties, during which guests typically stand, many more guests can be accommodated in the same space than at a sit down dinner because not that many chairs are needed. Once the banquet manager and the client have determined the number of guests expected to attend and the type of setup desired, the manager can decide which room can accommodate the group comfortably and efficiently.

Tables for Setting Banquet Functions

The manager knows the capacity of all the rooms and the

types of functions that may be booked into each room. The next thing the banquet manger needs to know are the types and sizes of tables available, so the function can be planned with comfort for the guests and efficiency for the banquet establishment.

Round tables: Round tables are used to create a jovial atmosphere. They should always be used when the client wants a function where fun and enjoyment are among the key ingredients for the success of the party. Round tables are a must for wedding receptions to encourage conversation. Most banquet houses use one of two sizes of round tables. The standard round table is 60 inches in diameter. This will seat eight people comfortably at a meal. The other size is 72 inches, which seats ten. The main disadvantage of a banquet facility using round tables is that round tables take up more space than rectangular tables. Therefore, the banquet facility cannot seat as many people at a function using round tables as it could using rectangular tables.

Oblong or rectangular tables: The three basic sizes of oblong or rectangular tables. They are 30 inches wide by 96 inches long (called an 8-foot table); 18 x 96 inches (8-foot by 1½-foot, or skinny); and 30 x 72 inches (6-foot). Each guest needs 24 inches of linear space to be comfortable. Therefore, an 8-footer will seat eight people (four on each side of the table).

The 6-footer will accommodate six people, and the 8 x 1½-footer will only accommodate four people. The skinny table is used when guests have to sit on one side of the table (at a head table or for a schoolroom style setup).

Eight foot by one-and-a-half foot tables can also be used for a block table. A block table is made by putting rectangular tables together to form a solid or hollow setup.

This style of setup is used when all participants want to be abie to see and communicate directly with each other. It is usually used at a meeting, but it can also be used for a small business dinner.

Space between tables: When guests are seated back to back, which is the case when rectangular tables are used, it is recommended that 60 inches are allowed between tables. Using round tables, 54 inches of space is allowed. Chairs are placed in the 60 inches and 54 inches of space. However, this is another area in which the banquet manager should experiment by actually setting up the rooms to determine if there is enough space between tables for the guests to be comfortable and for the service personnel to do their job efficiently. When doing this experiment, the banquet manager should instruct the person setting up the chairs not to push them under the tables but to keep them pulled out as if a guest were sitting at the table. The banquet manager will soon discover the capacity of the function rooms in the establishment.

Special-shaped tables: The trapezoid, serpentine, quarter—and half—round tables are best used for setting up food or bar stations rather than for the guests' dining. A banquet manager and chef can create an interesting food setup using the different shaped tables.

Lecterns: Lecterns are places in the centre of the head table and take up 24 inches (the same amount of space that a guest requires). On the lectern there is a place for the notes of the guest speaker, a light, and a microphone.

Podium: A podium serves the same purpose as a lectern. The difference between the two is that a podium is freestanding, while the lectern sits on the table. It also takes up 24 inches of space.

Microphone: Every banquet manager has to be aware of the types of microphones available for use in the function room. The banquet manager should know where the power source is for the microphone outlet, how to turn the system on, adjust the volume, and eliminate annoying feedback. One common mistake most people make when testing a microphone is not setting the volume loud enough.

The microphone system should be tested before the guests arrive in the function room. Often, the person testing the system does not take into account that there will be many more people in the room when the system is in use. A room with four hundred guests will produce a higher decibel volume of miscellaneous sounds than one with no guests; so the microphone must sound loud when it is being tested.

Audiovisual equipment: Most banquet facilities have movie screens, and some may have slide projectors. Other facilities have state-of-the-art rear projection systems. Regardless of the type of equipment the establishment owns, the banquet manager needs to know how to operate it. If a guest makes a request for equipment that the facility does not own, the banquet manager can rent it. Therefore, a knowledge of where to obtain the rental audiovisual equipment is needed, as must the amount of money to charge the guest for the rental.

Planning the Function Room

Every banquet manager must realise that planning the correct setup of a function room can be an integral part of the success or failure of a business meeting or party. There are a couple of facts that have to be stressed about equipment and use of function rooms. Especially important is the fact that all equipment room and thoroughly tested before the guests arrive.

For example, if the slide projector is rented, the banquet manager should have extra bulbs available, and know how to change bulbs if one burns out during a slide presentation. If the equipment is owned by the establishment, a regular maintenance schedule should be set up for changing bulbs so there will be no problem during the presentation. All equipment must be in working condition and ready to operate when the guests walk in. The second fact that the banquet manager must consider has to do with the placement of different types of functions in the rooms.

Many modern facilities have large function rooms that can be made into smaller rooms by the use of moveable walls. Many times these walls are not as soundproof as the manufacturer claims. A banquet manager would be wise not to place a business meeting in the same place as a wedding reception, with only the wall separating them. The banquet manager can play an integral part in the success or failure of a party by the planning and use of equipment. Practice, common sense, and the banquet manager's experience will benefit all the guests. This will result in more repeat business for the establishment. However, sometimes the banquet manager will get some unusual requests for equipment. When scheduling a function the banquet manager should see to it that there is enough space to accommodate all the guests comfortably in the room. There is one exception to this rule. Often clients who plan this exception to the rule want to schedule space that is much too small for the number of people that is expected at the event.

Physically Set up

Once the banquet manager knows the proper manner for setting up and the use of the function rooms, the next step is to physically set up the rooms for the function. The banquet manager should not set up the rooms. However, he or she should know how to diagram the function so the setup people will be able to accomplish the task without asking any questions. Most of the time, the people who have the responsibility of setting up the rooms are entry level workers. If they are trained properly (generally the banquet manager's job), they become excellent employees and are a valuable asset for the banquet manager. It is the banquet manager's responsibility to diagram all parties as requested by the client. This prepared diagram is then given to the setup people so they can physically set up the room.

The setup for a wedding reception for 198 guests. There is a key on the bottom of the diagram. All tables are clearly marked with their sizes, and there is a sample table for the setup person to follow. The head table has the exact specification of how many guests should be seated and where they should be seated. The key tells exactly how many tables, their sizes, and the number of chairs the setup people need to do their job. Because most setups are done during the night when the banquet manager is not working, the diagrams should be as complete as possible. In the morning, the first thing the banquet manager will do is check the rooms to make sure they are set up correctly. If there is a problem, it can be corrected, and it can be determined whether the mistake was the setup person's or the banquet manager's. The banquet manager must know how to diagram function rooms simply and concisely.

Booking of Functions

Once the banquet manager knows the capacity and use of the function rooms, the next task is to book functions. The booking of functions is done by a sales, catering, or banquet manager, or by a secretary. The title banquet manager will encompass all of these job titles. The banquet manager has to know exactly what types of meals, accommodations for meetings, and charges for these services the establishment can offer to the client. Usually this information is provided by the owners or the general manager of the establishment after the food has been costed out and the profit margin is added into the meal.

Most banquet managers work from a set price menu; caterers usually do not. Caterers set their prices based upon a variety of factors, such as what the client desires, the location of the party, day of the week, and how much demand there is for the caterer's services. Knowing all of this information, the booking process can begin.

To avoid the above situation, every facility must have an organised system to keep its bookings straight. In the past, the tool to use was a function book. Today, the function book is being replaced with computer software. However, whether a banquet establishment uses a function book or a computer, the basic principles are the same. A function book is an organised piece of equipment that lists the rooms that the establishment has to rent on a daily basis.

Each meal period and each day of the year are in the book. In addition, every room would be listed in the book. The person doing the booking would open the page to the date and see if anything was booked into the room. If there was nothing entered, then the booking person could sell the space to the guest. If there are no open dates or if the client cannot change the requested date, the banquet manager may make suggestions or even assist the client in finding another banquet facility that is comparable in service and price. This practice is beneficial to the banquet manager in a couple of ways. First, the client will be impressed that the banquet manager is taking the time to assist in finding an alternative banquet establishment. Second, the competition will reciprocate when it is booked up.

The function book does not provide any information about the menu or the party; only who reserved the room, whether it is a firm or tentative booking, and the approximate time and number of guests that will attend the function. The main purpose of the system is to avoid overbooking, which is defined as having two parties in the same room at the same time.

Because the function book is such an integral part of the banquet business, it should be kept in a permanent place. It should not be brought into another office or to a person's home when booking a party. When no one is in the office it should be kept in a locked area. The banquet facility must make certain that only authorised people are allowed to make entries into the book. All entries must be made in pencil, and the people who book the parties must identify themselves by putting their initials in the entry. One advantage computer software has over the traditional function book is that backup copies of all bookings can be saved and/or printed. There has always been a fear that if the book was stolen, lost, or damaged by fire, it would be difficult to reconfirm the bookings, and thus, overbooking would occur.

Policy Determination

Each banquet establishment has to set up a policy to determine the amount of money that must be made when a room is booked. Once that determination and policy has been set, the banquet manager should attempt to book parties that will bring in the most revenue for the establishment. Some banquet establishments will accept any and all business while others attempt to specialise in certain market areas, such as the social business. Qualifying a client means to determine how much money the client will be spending at the establishment. There is minimal space available. If a room is available for fifty guests, we are going to try to find a client that has an open-bar, extensive hors d'oeuvres, high revenue dinner, and possibly wine sales, in comparison to a cash bar and a chicken dinner.

The second part of qualifying means to determine if the client can pay for the party. Some clients have booked parties with no intention of paying for them. Unfortunately, this is usually people running for political office. It is best to make candidates pay for their functions in advance. There are many documented stories about candidates who have both won and lost elections, and still owe for their parties. The accepted method of payment should be explained to the client when the party is booked. The establishment has to decide if it will accept personal checks and/or credit cards, and how much of a deposit to charge the client. Once the business is qualified, the date can be entered into the function book as either a tentative or firm booking.

Each banquet facility has to determine, based upon the demand for space, a policy concerning how far in advance banquets may be booked. The goal of the facility is to obtain the most revenue. For example, a new banquet business would probably book any business, while one that is established and more in demand may set a limit on advance bookings.

Firm Booking

Bookings can be called either or firm. Firm bookings are the easiest to understand. A client gives the banquet manager a deposit for a party. Once the establishment receives the client's money and in some banquet establishments a signed contract for the event, the amount and date of the deposit, as well as the word firm, is entered into the function book. Tentative policy usually means that the banquet manager will put the client's name into the function book, and the client will have first refusal if another person calls and wants the same room at the same time. Again, a policy is established by the banquet facility and tentative bookings. At many banquet establishments tentative can mean that the space is held tentatively without a deposit for one week. After the week, the person who booked the party will call the client and ask if tic or she is still interested in the date.

If the client is still interested, a deposit must be brought in. The person who books the function writes in the book the term Firm, with the date and the amount of the deposit received. If the client does not bring the deposit within one week, he or she is called and informed that the deposit must be brought in before the close of business that day or the function will be cancelled. Banquet managers find that some dates are more particular than others. Often, the manager will have a tentative booking and then a client will come in a day later with a deposit for a firm booking. The banquet establishment needs a policy to determine which party to take and which party to refuse.

Protection of Deposits

A deposit is required for almost all banquet events. The deposit protects both parties. The banquet house will not sell the date that the client has reserved to another client; while the client will not cancel the event without losing the money that has been put down for the event. Each banquet house should determine the amount of deposit that it will charge. It should be expensive enough to deter the client from cancelling the party, while moderate enough not to deter the guest from booking the party with the banquet house. As an example, one banquet facility requires $200 deposit for social events that occur in any month except December.

Different operations have different policies on refunding the deposits. Some will never refund a deposit; other places will refund the deposit if the party is cancelled four months prior to the event; still other banquet houses will not give back the deposit unless another group rebooks the date. Of course there are always circumstances in which the manager will have to determine if giving back or keeping the deposit would be in the best interests of the business.

When booking functions, clients should be informed of the policy on guarantees of the establishment. A guarantee is a promise made by the host of the party that a certain number of guests will show up for the party and that the client will pay for that number unless more guests attend. When a client originally books an event, he or she gives an estimate of how many people will attend the party. Most banquet establishments require that the guarantee must be given three or four days prior to the event. Most establishments will take that number and set up 5 percent above that guaranteed number (one hundred guaranteed, 105 seats). The client pays for a minimum of one hundred people unless more guests show up.

Clients will be using the function rooms for food and beverage functions or meetings. There are different ways to charge for room rentals. If a client has a food and beverage function in a room, one for a meeting and one for a food and beverage function, the client may be charged the full price for the meeting room. Naturally, if a client uses just a meeting room, the full price for the meeting room is charged. At times, meeting room charges can be waived if the client spends additional money at the facility. For instance, if a client has booked two hundred rooms at a hotel, the meeting room charge is waived.

10

TRAINING TO SERVE THE MEAL

The dining room manager should insist that all employees know all the information about items on the menu. Employees should know which foods or beverages are offered, their pronunciation, and their ingredients. It is the responsibility of the manager to prepare this information for the employees. The information must be clearly written in a manual and given to all of the employees.

The waitress moved the menus and place settings to the new table. She then asked for their orders. They ordered salad and asked her what the salad dressing choices were. She said she didn't know because that was her first night on the job, though she had worked at the restaurant during the summer, before she went away to college. She asked the waitress next to her for the choice of salad dressings and then repeated them back to the guests. One of the guests was reading her menu and did not hear the choices. When she ordered her salad, the whole process had to be repeated, with their waitress again asking the other waitress the choice' of salad dressings.

Five of the six meals were delivered to the table. The order for the first guest (the hamburger) was served on a bun. There were three other meals, besides the hamburger, which were to receive French fries as an accompaniment. Each meal had on the plate, the sandwich, an orange garnish and a sprig of parsley, plus a large area of white space left on the plate. Five minutes later, the waitress brought a community basket of French fries to the table, explaining that they had not been ready when she had brought out the other food. The sixth meal was finally brought to the table along with the French fries.

Coffee was asked for and brought. The coffee was served with a napkin between the cup and saucer. The coffee spilled all over the napkin. The waitress asked the customer if she wanted a new napkin. The customer felt like saying "No, I'd rather slop it over my dress."

Service Person Should Know

Before a manager allows employees to wait on guests, there are many facts they should know. The first group of facts deals with specific policies about the restaurant. Acceptable standards of appearance, dress, and attendance should be explained before the service person has been hired. Additional items, such as what time to report to work, food and drink policies concerning consumption both on and off the job, and serving hours, should also be explained to the employees. These facts must be reinforced in a training booklet.

The next set of facts should deal with the establishment. The purpose of having these facts known is so the service people can answer any and all questions that guests ask. The guest will feel good about the service person if he or she is able to answer questions intelligently and confidently.

A third group of facts should be concerned with the physical layout of the restaurant. It should also explain how to order and pick up food and beverages. There should be an area that explains how to write and read guest dinner checks. The list is long but important for a successfully run restaurant.

Guests perceive service persons in two ways: Are they nice, and can they answer questions? Guests will ask many questions. Most of them are legitimate, but others may seem silly. However, they are not silly to the guest. All of the employees must know the history of the business. For example, questions will be asked concerning the ownership of the restaurant; how long has it existed; and what are the names and locations of other restaurants in the chain.

Other facts employees should know are the days and hours of operation of their restaurant. If there are any other restaurants on the premises or in the hotel, the employees should know their hours of operation, type of foods served, the general price range, and the dress code. There should be a daily listing stating what events are occurring in the restaurant, hotel, and community.

The manager should stress to the employees the correct way to write and read a guest check. The manager must translate all the menu items into standard abbreviations. Each item must have its own abbreviation.

All employees (including kitchen staff) are required to know and use the abbreviations when ordering food from the kitchen or serving food. This is to prevent any confusion in the restaurant. For example, what does SS on the check mean? Would the guest receive shrimp scampi, sirloin steak, or swiss steak? Abbreviations are used for all menu items, including accompaniments.

Many times restaurants offer a children's menu. With the advent of computerized systems, which transmit orders directly to the kitchen, does a service person still need to know the importance of using abbreviations? Yes. It will help the service staff know which guest gets which meal, for one thing. Also, in the case of an electronic or computer failure, the service staff should know how to use this method.

Knowledge about Menu

Many times guests are not familiar with your menu, so they ask the service person about the entrees. For example, a guest will ask "What is the shrimp scampi?" The service person should know the names of all items, how to pronounce them, and how to describe them. The training manual should have a description of all menu items.

Cooking Methods

Guests often inquire about terms on the menu that are unfamiliar to them. For instance, a guest may ask the meaning of saute. Each employee should know the more common preparation methods of cooking foods. There are at least twelve methods. This information is also needed in the manual. An example of two cooking methods: Baked-cooked by dry, continuous heat in an oven; sauteed-browned or cooked in a small amount of hot fat.

A chart of the cooking times of all menu items should be listed. The chart should range from Pittsburgh to well done, with the normal cooking time for each item.

Alcoholic Beverages

As with the food, there should be a description of every beverage the restaurant has available. In addition, there should be a description of how the drinks are made, the glass the drink is served in, and the proper garnish. The brand names of all wines and beverages must also be included in the section on alcoholic beverages.

Pricing

Because menus are constantly being changed, a separate price sheet should be distributed with the current prices. Owing to the fluctuation of prices, putting prices into the manual would be a waste of time and money. The prices will most likely change more often than any other information in the manual. When done on a separate sheet, the manager only has to print the new prices instead of the entire manual.

Tasting

This is another part of the training for the service staff that must be continuous. However, many restaurant managers refuse to let their staff taste the food. Instead, they serve them an employee meal each evening. The feeling is that it is too expensive to serve to the staff. In reality, it is too expensive not to serve it to the staff. The guests are going to ask the service person how the food tastes. If they have never been allowed to sample the food, how will your service staff know what to tell the guests?

The service staff should taste all food and beverage items as soon as it is practical. This does not mean that each night, the service staff should have a gourmet meal; but they must taste the food that they will be recommending and serving to their guests. One way of accomplishing this is by having meetings where the service staff sample the menu items. Or management could encourage the service staff to entertain their families at the restaurant and purchase their meals at a discount. Once the service staff has mastered the knowledge concerning the restaurant and menu by the testing criteria set up, it is time for them to move on to the second part: serving the meal.

Merchandising

Merchandising food and beverage is simply another term for selling. Selling occurs because the guest likes and is confident in the service person's ability. This part of the training programme should concentrate on getting the guests to like your staff. This should be done by placing the service staff in common situations that occur daily in the restaurant. This is called role playing. For instance, have the service staff ask the "guests" what type of salad dressing they want, using the example of the problem stated on the preceding page.

The service person should assess the mood of the guests as they approach the table. Are they celebrating and in a festive mood or do they appear somber, as if they have just returned from a funeral? Once the service person has assessed the situation, the behaviour should be appropriate for the situation.

Each guest deserves and expects a warm, sincere greeting. If the staff person knows the guest, the guest should be addressed by name. Furthermore, the staff should acknowledge the presence of the guest immediately and take care of any requests as soon as possible. This will make the guest feel as if the restaurant appreciates his or her patronage and will help make the dining experience a positive one.

Many times guests will know exactly what food they wish to order; other times they cannot make up their minds. There is a trick that experienced service persons use to sell items and help guests make up their minds. If guests are asked for their order and they hesitate, count backwards from seven. If the guests have not made up their minds by the time the server reaches zero, then they need help. And that opens it up for the service staff to sell suggestively.

The first step in suggestive selling is having the guests like the service person. Once this happens, the guests will respond to the service person's suggestions. The guests now trust the service person's knowledge and judgement. He or she has answered all the guests' questions about the restaurant, told them what is happening in the area, and is perceived as knowledgeable.

The service person may then describe a meal that tastes and looks great based upon their preference. This is the main reason why employees should be required to taste all items on the menu. They are then able to describe how the food tastes and can base their recommendations on what the guest desires.

The key to suggestive selling is for the service person to keep a positive attitude. The staff must put themselves in their guests' place, then use mouth-watering descriptions of the menu item for the purpose of selling the item. The service person shouldn't say, "Would anyone care for dessert?" Instead, he or she should describe the desserts available.

If a service person does not suggest desserts, or merely asks the' guests if they care to see a dessert menu, too often the answer is "No." By suggesting a specific dessert and using mouth-watering descriptions, the rate of success of selling desserts will be greatly enhanced. Another technique used by experienced salespeople is to suggest last the item they wish to sell. This is because people usually remember the last thing said to them.

Suggestive selling can build the profits for the restaurant by encouraging guests to order extra items that they normally would not have ordered. It also builds up the check total; and as most guests tip on the total bill, the amount of tip for the service person increases.

Service in Special Day

If you are shopping in a supermarket or for clothes, a special means reduced prices for that item. Does a special in the restaurant mean reduced prices? Contrary to that, it usually means a special item prepared by the chef. The price is special. In some areas it is lower priced, or "best buy," and in other areas it is higher than a normal menu item. A manager might do well to change the name of the special of the day to the chef's creation. Then the service staff can approach the table and explain the chef's creation to the guests. Should the service staff be instructed to inform the guests of the price of the chef's creation?

No one has ever satisfactorily explained the reason why prices are not given when a special item is offered. This is another positive factor that builds up the trust of the guest. Another annoying custom is for restaurants to instruct their service staff to offer an item (such as blue cheese dressing), and state it is "a la carte." Most guests have no idea what a la carte means. The service staff should inform the guests the price of all items.

Other techniques may assist the service staff in selling additional items in a restaurant. These are usually associated with wine and dessert sales. More and more restaurants include wine glasses at the place setting. Others sell a sample two-ounce portion of wine to the guests. Still others put a bottle of unopened wine on each table to encourage guests to order wine with their meal.

Desserts provide the opportunity to increase sales enormously. Even though the American public is becoming more nutrition conscious and eating lighter meals, survey after survey has found that guests will order desserts. Many restaurants display their desserts so the guests can view them before they begin their meal. This technique has been used successfully by many restaurants for merchandising desserts. If the desserts are kept attractive and eye-appealing, the guest will usually order dessert. However, if the cart or table becomes messy and unappetizing, it does the restaurant more harm than good.

Another excellent way to merchandise desserts is to bring out a sample tray of all desserts. The service person brings the trays to the guests' table and describes the desserts to them. This method eliminates the problem of the desserts looking unattractive, because the desserts on the tray are not served to the guests. Instead, the service person obtains the desserts from the kitchen. As soon as a dessert on the tray looks unappealing, it is replaced.

One of the best selling gimmicks that has been used for ages is initiated by the manager. If done properly, it can increase sales and repeat business dramatically. It involves the manager giving away an item that will call attention to that item. For example, a restaurant sells flaming coffee. The manager should approach a table in the center of the dining room, where other guests can see the coffee being prepared.

The manager should introduce himself or herself to the guests, inquire about their meal, thank them for their business, and offer to buy them an after dinner coffee. Once the coffee is being prepared, all, the eyes in the dining room are attracted to the coffee presentation. This display will encourage other guests to order the coffee after their meals. This can be done with a fancy dessert, large glass of beer, or any type of fancy entree. The cost of this to the restaurant is the cost of the item. In addition, the guest will feel special, because the manager gave away an item.

The manager must encourage the service staff to sell extra items. The guests have already made the decision to patronize the restaurant. With suggestive selling, the service staff can increase profits for the restaurant. However, one word of caution: the manager must make certain that the service staff do no push so hard that the guests become upset with their selling aggressiveness and have a bad dining experience.

Order Taking

Training your staff to take a guest's food and beverage order correctly is critical. There are many correct methods to take the order. All of them should have one goal: to serve the meal to the guest without having to ask who gets what. The manager should teach the service staff how to talk to the guests and how to take meal orders.

The manager must impress upon the service staff that they should treat the guests as if they had never dined at the restaurant before. They do not know how the specials are made or what the salad dressing is that evening. It must be impressed upon the service staff that this will be the first time the guest hears the specials. Even though the service staff may have repeated them one hundred times that evening, employees should be taught to explain every item to each guest.

The manager must train staff to explain in detail the chef's creation of the evening. When it is time to offer the guest the choice of salad dressings or vegetables, explain what they are. Rather than let the staff say, "And what would you like on your salad?" encourage them to say something like: "A salad is included in the meal. Our choice of dressings are: blue cheese; Russian; Italian; and our house dressing, which is a sweet and sour dressing made with mustard and honey." The same should be true for vegetables, potatoes, and chef creations, especially if the item is new or one that is not normally served in the area where your restaurant is located. Included in the explanation can be the ingredients, how it is prepared, and the price.

Finally, the order should be repeated back to the guest. By doing this, your service staff will avoid any misunderstandings of guest orders. However, the method used should not be annoying to the guests. For instance, a service person who echoes every single item that the guest orders will be annoying. It is much better to wait until the complete order is taken and then repeat the main course back to the guest.

The job of the service staff should not just be to serve the food, but to be the human link between the kitchen and the guest. This is why the importance of verbal communication between the service staff and the guest must be stressed. It gives the restaurant a personality.

Service Person Should Stand

There are two opinions on where the service persons should be standing when they take the guests' order. Both agree that order taking should follow the proper guidelines of service: children first, then women, then men. There is an exception, when one person is the host of the party and he or she is ordering for the entire table.

The first method states that the service person should stand to the left of the guest and take the order, then move to the next person, following the proper guidelines of service, and take the order. The problem with this method is that if the service person takes the order by following proper guidelines, it may be necessary to skip over one male guest to take the next female's order. The service person will then have to return to the man, and move back and forth, creating much unnecessary confusion.

The second method is to have the service person stand in one spot and take all the guests' orders from that spot, following the proper guidelines of service. This works well at a table with two to four guests. However, for more than four guests, especially with rectangular-shaped tables, the service person may have to move to different spots in order to hear the order.

Whichever method is used, the management should set guidelines for their own restaurant, keeping in mind that guests should be served smoothly and efficiently.

How to write the Guest Orders

Once the staff know where the home base is, the next thing the manager must teach them is how to write the guest orders. The system must be explained simply enough so that any employee who picks up the food order can deliver it to the guests without having to ask who gets what. Each person should be provided with some sort of form with which to take orders. The service person must be organized; but it is up to the manager to devise this policy in such a way that all employees will know who gets what item.

Some restaurants use a system that has the guest check remain at the table, in a slot provided in each table. The duplicate check (dupe) is brought into the kitchen to order the food. The guest check can have the system of "who gets what" directly written on the check. The service staff will write the check in the following manner: The seat immediately to the left of the slot is the number 1 seat. Going in a clockwise direction, the seats are numbered consecutively, 2, 3, 4. The management arranges the tables so that the slots are always in the same position relative to the home base.

These are two methods for writing guest orders and determining who gets what order. There are other methods, but they all have one thing in common: They are set up in an organized manner than can be easily learned. The key is to have the manager decide on one system and have all of the staff use the same system.

Code Order System

Another system for determining who gets what is the code order. This system is not recommended, because too much confusion and embarrassment can result. The code order system was used in the past when a single service person was responsible for the station. The service person would write next to the order a code to identify the guest. The code would represent some distinguishing feature that made one guest stand out from the other, such as blue tie or red hair. This system can create problems because not all the service staff would understand the system. It also could be embarrassing if the service person uses a code order that was derogatory toward the guestsuch as fat person, bald, or grey hair.

Ordering in the Kitchen

Correct ordering in the kitchen is a must for guests to receive their dinner cooked and served properly. As the service staff know the time it takes to cook every item, they should submit their orders based on the mood of the guests and how long it will take to cook the meal. In most restaurants, the time to submit the order is when the service person picks up the guests' salad from the kitchen. In restaurants with a salad bar, the service person is instructed to turn the order into the kitchen when the guests go to obtain their salads from the salad bar. However, each manager can determine what is best for his or her individual unit.

Depending on the type of system, the service persons may be required to order all the entrees at the top of their check. They may put all the cold items at the bottom. Others may have a computerized system that prints all the orders in a priority based on cooking times. It does not matter how it is done, as long as all members of the staff use common abbreviations and the same system.

Serving the Meal

This is the critical part of the meal. If the meal is served incorrectly, the evening can be ruined. The service staff has ordered the meal correctly. It has been cooked properly, and the kitchen is waiting for the service person to serve it to the guest in the dining room. But instead of being picked up and delivered to the guest, it sits in the kitchen, becoming colder and less appetizing. Timing is of the essence. The staff must get the meal to the table as soon as it is ready. If the dinners sit too long, the quality suffers, and the guests become impatient. More and more restaurants are using electronic means to notify the service person that the meal is ready.

These electronic devices may include a light system, a vibrating beeper, or other methods to let the service person know that the order is ready to be picked up. As soon as the food is ready, the service person should pick it up and bring it to the table. But before doing so, the service person should take a few seconds to check that all the food items on the dupe match those that have been prepared by the kitchen. He or she must also check to see that all special instructions on the dupe have been followed. The tray will be loaded by placing the cold items first, then the hot items. The food on the tray should be arranged to serve the guests in the most efficient manner. Any condiments and garnishes should be brought to the guests' table along with the entrees.

The sequence for serving a typical meal using the team system is as follows:

1. All the sidework has been completed, the service staff are prepared to receive their guests. The service staff know the chef features of the day; what items are 86ed. They have their guest checks and duplicate order forms to take orders.

2. Guests are seated by the host, presented with menus, both food and wine. Chef features are recited or given out using a printed daily chef feature menu.
3. The Lead approaches the table, greets the guests in a friendly manner; answers questions about the menu, and offers to take drink or wine orders.
4. Drinks are written on the check and the order form, using the system that has been taught to all service staff. In the team system, the check never leaves the table. The check is placed back into the slot in the table.
5. Drinks are served on a cocktail napkin in the center of the setting. If the setting has a show or starter plate, the drink is placed on the center of the starter plate. All drinks are served from the right side of the guest with the service person's right hand.
6. The food order is taken by the Lead. The Lead attempts to merchandise the additional items. After the order is taken, the menus are collected by the Lead.
7. The order is placed on a duplicate check; the Lead holds it in his or her pocket until it is time to turn it into the kitchen to order food.
8. The Aid picks up the appetizer (first course) from the kitchen and serves it to the guests. When an appetizer is served and there has not been a piece of flatware included in the cover for an appetizer, it is brought with the food. For example, if a bowl of soup is served, the soup is served from the left side with the left hand, and the soup spoon is placed on the right side of the guest. The staff do not reach across the front of the guests but walk behind them to put the spoon in its proper location.
9. Rolls and butter are served by the Aid, who places them to in the center of the table

10. The first course is removed from the guest's right with the Aid's right hand,
11. Salad is served, or the guests go to the salad bar. If a guest requests salad dressing on the side, it is placed in a separate container and served on a bread and butter plate, called an underliner. The salad is placed in the center of the place setting or on the starter plate.
12. When salads are served, the Lead turns the check into the kitchen for the food to be cooked.
13. Wine is served at this point, or it was served as soon as it was requested. The Lead shows the label to the person who ordered the wine. Once the guest verifies that this is the wine desired, the Lead opens the wine and presents the cork to the guest. The guest should feel the cork (it should be wet) to determine if the wine was stored properly. The Lead then pours about an ounce into the glass of the guest. Once the guest approves of the wine, the Lead pours the wine into the glasses of the guests, using proper serving techniques. Glasses of red wine should be filled %2 full; white, 3/4 full. The bottle of red wine is placed on the table, while the white wine should be placed in an ice bucket.
14. Salad plates are removed, as well as the starter plate. If guests tell the service staff they would like to finish their salad with the meal, the staff person should move it to the left of the place setting.
15 When the food order is ready, the kitchen informs the Aid to pick up food by calling out section 1, or by following whatever its system might be for informing service staff when the food is cooked and; ready to be served.
16. The entree is picked up in the kitchen. The plates are placed in the same order as written on the duplicate check. The Aid compares the food to the duplicate

check. If any mistakes are found, they are corrected immediately. It is the responsibility of the person picking up the food to make certain that the plate is eye-appealing, attractive, and the proper temperature.

17 Before food is served to guests, the service person makes certain that plates are the proper temperature, attractive (no gravy or juices slopped on the rim of the plate), and garnished correctly.

18. All entrees are brought to the table together. If the service person has more entrees than can fit on the tray, another service person carries out the remaining food. All guests receive their food at approximately the same time; no one has to wait while the service person returns to the kitchen to pick up the additional meals.

19. The entree is served without asking who gets what. If vegetables or potatoes are served in a side dish (called monkey dishes), they are placed above and near the main entree dish. The staff never puts one course in front of the guest before the previous course has been removed. If a woman is not finished eating her salad when the service person removes the other salad dishes, her salad dish is removed before her entree is placed in front of her.

20. Condiments that accompany the main courses (such as sour cream, catsup, and so on) are placed on the guests' table.

21. All meat items are placed in front of the guest with the meatiest part facing the guest (meat in front), so when the guest cuts the meat, they cut into the most tender part. If starch and vegetables are served on the same plate, they are placed the farthest from the guest.

22. As soon as all entrees are served to the guests, the service person checks the table to determine if more rolls and butter are needed or if more wine is to be

poured, and inquires if there is anything else that the guests would like.

23. Throughout the meal, the Lead constantly checks the tables to determine if guests need more drinks. In order to save time, the Lead learns to take more than one table's order at once. Then the Lead can order ten or twelve drinks at once instead of having to make four separate trips back and forth.
24. The service staff check back at the table as soon as the guests sample their food to inquire if the food is done to their satisfaction. The question is not, "Is everything OK here?" because that assumes that it is not. Instead, it is "Is the steak cooked the way you ordered it?" Any problems are taken care of immediately. Food is returned to the kitchen and recooked if it is not done well enough. If food is done too well, the service person informs the guest that it will take extra time to cook the meal over and offers an alternative item that is already prepared and can be served immediately.
25. Once the guests inform the Follow-Up that the food is done to their satisfaction, the guest check is flipped over so the other members of the team can see that the table has been checked.
26. The service staff returns to the table to pour extra wine and water throughout the meal. Water glasses are filled as soon as they are half empty. Any time a service person performs any service at the table, he or she converses with the guests.
27. As soon as all guests have finished eating their meals, (the staff can determine this as guests put their utensils across their dinner plates or push their dinner plates away from them) their plates are removed.
28. If any guests have not finished their main course, an inquiry is made to determine if the guests would like

to have the remainder of the meal wrapped so they may take it home. If the answer is "Yes," the server takes one plate at a time to the sidestand to wrap the leftover food, and brings it back to the guest. This eliminates having the guest question whether the food they have received is their own. The service persons bring wrapping material with them when they are preparing to clear the dirty dishes.

29. The staff remove all the dirty dishes, including bread baskets, bread and butter plates, butter plates, dirty glasses, and wine glasses.
30. The service staff crumb the table with either the side towel or a crumbing device. The crumbs are swept into a bread and butter plate.
31. The staff inquire from the guests if they would like coffee or tea. They merchandise dessert by using descriptive words, such as "our triple chocolate dessert."
32. Coffee is served by the service person, using a coffee shield. Tea is served by placing the teapot above the coffee cup. Cream, sugar, and lemon are served with the tea and coffee,
33. Dessert is served to the guests. If one dessert is ordered for two people, the staff bring two forks. If the dessert is gigantic, they inform the guest, and bring extra plates for other guests to share the dessert.
34. The staff serve second and third cups of coffee and tea before the guests have to ask for additional beverages. Once the dirty entree, dishes have been cleared and the coffee and dessert served, the meal is not over? The guests deserve as much attention at the end of the meal as they receive at the beginning of the meal.)

35. The check is presented to the guests. If the staff cannot determine who is the host of the party, they place the check face down in the center of the table.
36. When the guests pay the bill, they are thanked for their patronage and encouraged to return.
37. After the guests leave, the staff reset the table for the next party of guests.
38. Throughout the meal, the service staff are always thinking of ways to save time. They never go into the kitchen empty-handed or come out empty-handed. They are attuned to when and how to change the ashtrays if the guests are smoking tobacco. The preceding illustrates a typical sequence of serving a meal using the team system. (However, this typical meal will work with any system.) Depending upon the restaurant's menu, steps may be changed to fit the individual needs of the operation.

Computer Terminals in Dining Room

There are many computer systems designed to make a restaurant more efficient. Some of these point of sale systems allow the server to transmit the order directly to the kitchen with a hand-held electronic order pad. Other systems have computer terminals throughout the dining room to allow the waitstaff to enter information to the kitchen.

All of the systems are a benefit for the guests, servers, and management. Traditional face-to-face service is being transformed by technology.

With the push of a button, the order is zapped to the kitchen, where it is printed out for the chef. The wireless ordering shaves as much at ten minutes off a meal. "We can handle more diners at night, because everything comes out faster" says Edward Saravia, the restaurant's general manager. And each waiter now handles a dozen tables a shift, twice the load handled before adopting the hand-held devices.

Other restaurants are using electronics to better address customer tastes. With technology becoming more affordable, independent restaurants can compete with chain operations. For instance, the Chilli's chain, owned by Brinker International, Inc., has instituted a frequent-diner programme. When a guest makes a purchase at a Chilli's, credits are placed toward free meals or prizes. The same type of programme has been put in place in independent restaurants.

As with any computer system, management must train the staff properly and the more a server uses the technology, the easier it is to understand. The computer has changed the way restaurants, managers, and servers do business.

Computerized point of sale (POS) systems save time for management in many ways-in taking inventory, making reports, handling accounting, cutting training time for wait staff, etc. It is easy to see that investment in a point of sale system is quickly repaid in saved labour costs, greatly reduced losses from inaccurate ordering, and enhanced security. Orders cannot be prepared or served until they are rung up, which occurs simultaneously upon ordering, thus protecting the establishment from the common losses incurred by such instances as forgetting to enter the sale of an item added after initial ordering.

Some systems have developed inventory control tied to the ordering process; the computer knows the ingredients in each item ordered and reports the depletion to its inventory database with every order entered. Special access cards are commonly used to allow managers to easily run reports, authorize a comp, or add employees by swiping the card's magnetic strip through the same slot that reads credit cards.

In choosing any type of computer equipment for a food service establishment, it is important to consider the practicality of the system for its environment. No industry could be more hostile to sensitive equipment. Sticky liquids, food crumbs, and multiple users will put the equipment to a daily durability test. Understandably, there is a great argument for choosing hardware developed specifically for the restaurant industry.

11

Planning Reservations and Blocking Tables

One of the most important considerations in not accepting reservations is the location of the restaurant. A restaurant that is located in an area where there is a large population, or in a busy tourist area, may prefer not to take reservations. A large population guarantees the restaurant the number of potential guests needed to fill up its tables. The same is true in a busy resort area that caters to tourists. If the establishment is located in the area where guests have to travel a long distance to reach it, this will be a negative factor. A second negative factor would be the absence of other restaurants of the same quality in the general area. The guest will take both of these factors into consideration, and most likely will not attempt to patronise the restaurant.

The next factor is the size of the party. Because most restaurants have the majority of their tables as deuces and 4-tops, they are not equipped to accommodate groups larger than six people. It would be difficult, if not impossible, to accommodate a group of ten people at one table. Imagine a busy night at a restaurant. All the tables are occupied. A large group appears at the door and wants to sit together. The host would have to wait until three tables next to each other become vacant all at once. Then the host would have to move the tables so they could accommodate the party.

To avoid this problem, reservations should be accepted for large parties. The definition of large would depend upon the size of the tables in the individual restaurant. Usually, large is a party of six or more guests. Reservations should always be accepted on holidays. Easter and Mother's Day are special days for families. The families want to be assured that they can arrive at a restaurant, enjoy themselves, pay the bill, and leave in a definite period of time. For many people, it is the only time of the year that all members of the family can have a meal together.

ADVANTAGES AND DISADVANTAGES OF RESERVATIONS

Some establishments only reserve a certain percentage of tables. Many restaurants prefer the restaurant to be reserved completely. A gourmet restaurant like Victoria and Albert's Restaurant in Walt Disney World's Grand Floridian Beach Resort only takes reservations. A reservation is a promise for a table in a restaurant. The promise works in two ways. The restaurant promises to have a table available for the guest for a certain time period. The guest promises to show up for': the reservation. Reservations provide a mutual benefit to the guest and the restaurant. The guests know that they will have a table available to enjoy their meal. They will not have to wait for their table, or even worse, drive to the restaurant and find out they cannot be accommodated. Reservations have advantages and disadvantages for both the restaurant and guests. The benefits for the guests:

— The table is available when requested.

— The restaurant can be informed of special requests and have them available when guests arrive.

— The host learns the guests' names.

The benefits for the restaurant:

— The restaurant knows how many guests to expect; forecasting and scheduling are easier.

— The menus and service staff can be planned exactly.

— The host knows guests' names and can use them to create ego gratification.

— A mailing list can be developed for future promotions.

— If reservations are taken correctly, the restaurant will run smoothly, because the restaurant controls when the guests dine. The restaurant can prevent too many guests from showing up at the same time, thereby avoiding a strain on the kitchen and dining room.

However, reservations can also be a disadvantage. Among the disadvantages for the guests:

— If restaurants do not know how to take and plan them correctly, reservations may not be honoured at the stated time.

— Some restaurants reserve more parties than they have tables available. This practice is called overbooking. The restaurant does this to avoid losing revenue in case guests who have reservations do not show up. Others overbook because they do not know how to plan reservations.

The possible disadvantages for the restaurant:

— When guests do not show up (called no-shows), revenue from that reserved table is lost.

— When guests arrive late, the reservation plan may be put in disarray.

— Restaurants that do not know how to block tables correctly lose money because they are not getting maximum use from tables.

Taking reservations are a benefit to the guest and the restaurant only if both know their responsibilities concerning reservations. Training the host in the proper way to take reservations is important. When guests make a reservation, it is an essential part of the host's job to explain to the caller their responsibilities. As was stated in the list of disadvantages for the guests, one of the main problems is overbooking by the restaurant. The first thing that will have to be established by management is a system that allows the people taking reservations to know exactly how many tables can be reserved for the day. Also, if the restaurant takes more than one seating for the meal period, the residence time has to be established. The residence time is defined as the time it takes a party to eat its meal and pay its bill.

For example, ninety minutes will be required for a complete meal with appetisers, drinks, main course, and dessert for a party of up to four people. Thus, leaving enough time to reset the table, reservations should be taken every two hours. Guests who have larger parties will take longer to eat, so the residence time must be adjusted. Other factors also influence the residence time of the guests. Items such as music, lighting, decor, mood, ambience, and special events make the difference in how fast or slow the guests will eat. A menu that is easier to prepare will speed up the residence time. Once the residence time and the system have been developed, the host can take reservations.

Competent in Taking Reservations

Practically all reservations are taken via the telephone or in person. The people taking the reservation have to be trained properly so they will obtain all important information from the guests and explain to them the policies of the restaurant. The person answering the phone must be competent in taking reservations, but also must have excellent telephone courtesy. This is the guest's first contact with the restaurant. To ensure this, management may check their reservation procedures by conducting mystery calls to determine the telephone courtesy and competency of the host. It is common telephone courtesy for the people answering the phone to identify the restaurant as well as themselves. A sentence such as this is appropriate: "Good day, thank you for calling the Speciality restaurant; this is Sue speaking, how may I help you?" This depends entirely on the size of the restaurant. A small restaurant would be able to put the reservations directly into a book. A large restaurant would have to use forms and then transfer them to the book afterwards. Some restaurants use personal computers with software developed to manage the reservation process. Regardless of what type of form the restaurant uses, the information required from the guest is generally the same.

Information from the Guest

The Name of the guest: Included in this step is the correct spelling of the guests' names.

The Date for Which the Reservation is Desired: Ask for the date that they request with the day of the week and date: For example, when the guests state, April 2, reconfirm it by saying, "Saturday, April 2." If the date is open, proceed with other questions. If the date is booked, suggest a different day. If the guests are adamant and insist on that date, take the guests' names and phone numbers and tell them they will be placed on the waiting list. Depending upon the restaurant, there should be a maximum number of parties that can be on the waiting list. Inform them that they will be called if an opening occurs.

The Time of the Reservation: If the time is booked, suggest other times. At this point, the host should explain the policy concerning holding reservations. For example, a restaurant may have the policy that when guests make a reservation they are told they must be at the restaurant fifteen minutes early. It is further explained to the guest that if their reservation is for 6 P.m., they must show up at 5:45. If the guest is not there at 5:45, the table is given to a walk-in.

Obtain the Number of Guests in the Party and any Special Requests: If they need a birthday cake, special seating, or anything else, this should be noted.

Ask for the Guest's Phone Number: Take both the home and business numbers, if possible. If there is a problem, the host can contact the guests. The host may want to contact them after the meal to find out how they liked their dining experience.

There are other items that the person taking the reservations should place on the reservation form. By placing these items on the form, they can be used in case any problems arise, as well as for planning future reservations.

The Name of the Person Who Took the Reservation: The people who booked the party must sign their names. This makes people responsible, and if a problem arises, the host will know whom to ask. If the guest calls and changes the reservation in any way, the person who took the changes must also sign and date the reservation request form.

The Date the Reservation was Taken: Noting the date on which reservations have been taken allows the host to determine how far in advance reservations are demanded.

Before the person taking the reservation thanks the guest and hangs up the phone, the guest will appreciate being informed of any special policies of the restaurant. For example, if the restaurant requires jackets for men in the dining room, this is told to the guest. The guest can be told that a gratuity is automatically added to the check. Each restaurant should develop its own checklist for reservation takers to make certain that the guest is informed of all of the policies.

Advantages for the Restaurant

When factors warrant not taking reservations, the advantages for the restaurant are much greater than for the guest. (Many no-reservation restaurants will take reservations for larger groups-usually six or more.) There are four main advantages for the restaurant.

— *Maximum use of tables is obtained*: Many restaurants that accept reservations will lose the use of tables for a period of time, because the host reserves the tables incorrectly. For example, if a party of ten has a reservation for 8:30 P.m., the host puts three tables together and sets the table up at 5 P.m. Those tables are lost for the first three-and-a-half hours. Even when the host reserves tables correctly, some time will be lost. When tables are not occupied because the table is reserved, and other guests are waiting for a table, a reservation policy loses money for the restaurant and service staff. With a no-reservation policy, the guests are seated on a first-come basis and the restaurant is not losing money from unoccupied tables.

— *No Overbooking Occurs*: With a no-reservation policy, there is no danger of reserving more tables than the restaurant has to accommodate the guests.

— *Little Pre-planning of Reservations is Needed*: The host only reserves tables for large parties. At all other times, the host will seat the guests at any table that is available.

— *No-Shows Are Not a Problem*: Because reservations are not accepted (except for large parties), there is no danger of holding a table and not having the guest show up to use the table. Even if the large party fails to show up, the host can reset the tables and accommodate the guests waiting for a table.

There are a couple of disadvantages for the restaurant that has a no reservation policy:

— Business may be lost because reservations will not be accepted.

— Guests may refuse to patronize the restaurant because they believe they will have to wait for a table for a long period of time.

Both of these disadvantages have to do with the attitude, convenience, and beliefs of the guests. Many guests do not want to wait for a table. They want to be assured that they will have a table when they arrive at a restaurant. If reservations are not taken, the guest may decide to go to another restaurant where accommodations can be secured without waiting for a table. The second disadvantage occurs after the restaurant has been in business for some time. The restaurant is a success and it attracts a large volume of business. The wait for a table becomes longer than an hour. The word of mouth network that the public uses so well informs other potential guests of this fact.

This works negatively for the restaurant. Many people will not want to wait that long, so they do not try to get into the restaurant. Eventually, because so many people decide to go to other restaurants, the amount of business decreases. However, the belief that the restaurant still has a long time for a wait persists in the community, even though it might not be true. In a no-reservation system, the disadvantages for the guest far outweigh the advantages. There are no outstanding advantages for the guest. It might be argued that everyone has the same opportunity of obtaining a table; however, it is a common practice in many no-reservation establishments to "push" regular customers to the top of the waiting list.

The disadvantages for the guest are many. Most of them have been stated already. Two more disadvantages:

— The guests have to wait for a table; a large party may experience an extended wait if the restaurant does not take any reservations.

— If the guests are planning some other event besides dinner (such as the theatre), there is no guarantee that they will be seated in time to attend.

Regardless of whether the restaurant has a reservation or no-reservation policy, knowing how to reserve tables is an integral part of the host's job. This is because all restaurants should take reservations on holidays and for large parties (usually, six or more guests).

BLOCKING RESERVATIONS

The term blocking means to reserve a certain table at a certain time for a guest. Its purpose is to enable the host to avoid overbooking. As was previously stated, each restaurant must determine the residence time for each meal period. Once this is known, the dining room can be blocked correctly. The process of blocking begins with taking the reservation correctly. Successful blocking depends upon an organised system. There are a few common procedures involved in all systems.

Regardless of the method that is used, all blocking is to be entered in one book or place, such as a three-ring binder. This is preferable to individual sheets of paper, which may get lost. The physical layout of the dining room (with tables and numbers) is designed and duplicated. Restaurants that have entered the computer age may block tables using a computer programme. However, all methods use the same basic principle: A table can only have one party reserved to use the table at each time period.

Blocking Tables

The simplest way of blocking tables occurs when a restaurant has set meal periods and a limited number of tables. In addition to the pre-printed reservation pad, all that is needed is a chart. Across the top of the chart is the day of the week and date. Obviously, the restaurant would have a different chart for each day of the week and for each meal period. The next line of headings shows table number, number of seats at each table, and the times of the reservations. This restaurant is only accepting reservations at 5:30 P.m. and 8 P.m. In this restaurant of six tables with twenty-two seats, there are only three unreserved tables. By using this form, the restaurant can avoid the problem of overbooking. All employees know exactly at all times how many tables can be reserved. When a guest desires a reservation, the host can turn to the date in the book to see if the party can be accommodated. Then all the information needed for a reservation can be obtained from the guest.

Without Set Meal Times

Some small restaurants will take reservations on a first-come, first seated basis. They will take reservations at any time during their meal period. First, the restaurant must know the residence time of the guests. This residence time is then incorporated into the planning for reserving tables. Second, the times that the restaurant will take reservations are stated in time segments at the top of the chart. Third, the guests' names must be written on the chart and their residence time blocked out. The residence time for their party of three is two hours. The restaurant can take another reservation at 8 P.m. What problems do you envision using this type of system? Will the restaurant obtain maximum use of the tables? This is another example of a system that works well for a small restaurant. But how will a large restaurant avoid overbooking?

First, a decision must be made whether to accept reservations at any time the guest desires or only at specified times that the restaurant sets. The principle of blocking tables in a large restaurant is the same as for a small restaurant, but it is impossible to block out reservations using the same method because of the large number of tables involved. There would be too much paperwork at the host's desk. The system in a large restaurant relies on having a person responsible for the planning and blocking of all reservations. This person is also responsible for informing those who take reservations about the number of tables left for each meal period. A large restaurant may have a person whose sole job is to be the reservation manager.

With Set Meal Times

This method of blocking tables requires four steps. It is referred to as the check-off method. The first thing that the manager determines is the number of tables available to be reserved in the restaurant. For example, a restaurant has four tables that seat six or eight; twelve tables that seat two; and sixteen tables that seat up to four. Seating and placed into the three-ring binder where the reservations are being recorded. Each seating has its own individual chart. The person taking the reservations checks off the size of the table that has been reserved.

The chart would continue to be crossed off and filled out until all the tables are used. If a guest desired a reservation larger than six or eight, the reservation manager would have to establish a policy for accepting or rejecting the request. As large parties require combining existing tables, the reservation manager must carefully plan for the large parties, or overbooking will occur. Each restaurant should decide the maximum number of large parties that can be accepted. A set formula has to be determined for checking off tables so the restaurant will not overbook.

For example, a reservation for twelve may include putting together four 4-tops and a deuce. When a reservation is made for a party of twelve, four 4-tops and a table for two must be crossed off. The reservation manager, to assist in the planning of reservations, will have a printed diagram of the dining room and will block the guests' names and time next to the table that they have been assigned. As more reservations arrive, the remainder of the dining room can be blocked off. The key factor in making this system work is to have constant communication between the reservation manager and the people taking the reservations.

Reserve Tables for Any Time

If the restaurant allows guests to reserve tables for any time (called open seating), then even more planning and organising must be done to avoid overbooking. The check-off sheet would be used, except that the sheet would have the guest's name and the time of the reservation. This informs all people taking reservations that the reservation is for 1 P.m. As the people taking reservations know that the usual residence time for a guest table is two hours, they may accept another reservation at 3 P.M. for the table.

However, this system could become very confusing when multiple reservations are made and/or for guests who come late or early or overstay the residence time. Therefore, the reservation manager would be advised to block out tables daily on the master chart of the dining room. Each day, an updated sheet should be put in the three-ring binder showing the number of tables left to reserve. It is easy to understand why a computer software programme that reserves seats would be ideal for a large restaurant.

Towards Effective Blocking

For the small restaurant, blocking is a simple process. Large restaurants create more of a challenge. Blocking involves much planning and organisation so that the guests will have their tables available when they arrive. In order to block effectively, the reservation manager needs three items: a diagram of the dining room, the reservations, and the check-off sheet. The diagram of the dining room must have the table number and the number of people that can be seated at each table. The reservations are the pre-printed forms that the person taking the reservations has completed. And the check-off sheet is the control sheet that was located where the reservations have been taken.

Blocking is accomplished by the way of an organised process. First, the reservation manager assigns the reservation to an appropriately-sized table. Finally, an alphabetised listing of the guests arriving is completed alongside their expected arrival time and their assigned table. From the list and a copy of the blocking diagram, it is easy for the host to know what tables are blocked and what guests are to be seated at which table. Because the reservations are set up first by time and then alphabetised, the host's job becomes easier, as much planning has taken place before the guest has arrived. The alphabetised reservation list.

After the reservation manager has blocked the tables, the guests' names are organised on a reservation form. This system works well if planned and executed properly. However, there are some problems that can be associated with this system. First, if the guests do not like the table they have been assigned, the host may have a problem with the guests. The host has a few options. For example, the guests' table could be switched to another comparable table. Or an apology could be offered and an explanation given why the guests cannot have the table they desire (e.g., all the other tables are reserved). If the host ever does switch a table for the guest, the master sheet also has to be updated. Second, if the guests stay beyond the residence time, the next party will have to wait for their table. Another problem that can occur is to have a party appear for their reservation and state that they have a few more people to add to the party. This can create a real headache for the restaurant. The host must calmly talk to the person in charge of the reservation and assure him or her that the restaurant will accommodate the party as soon as it is possible.

Next, the host should make whatever arrangements are necessary (add an extra seat to a table, put two tables together, etc.) to seat the guests. This is one of the situations in which the host has to use his or her good judgement, tact, and diplomacy to keep everyone happy: the guests, service staff, and other guests. Easter were running smoothly until 4 P.m. At that time, the staff began to get tired (both dining room and kitchen) and the residence time increased. Some guests had to wait for their assigned tables. As a solution, the hosts deviated from the plan, putting guests at tables that they were not assigned.

Guests were being brought to tables that should have been vacant and were not. The hosts could not keep up with the changes that were being made. Confusion reigned for those two hours. Fortunately, they learned from their mistakes. The restaurant's planning took into account the fatigue factor of the staff. It increased the residence time of the guests for later in the day and did not deviate from the plan. The result of the planning was that just one party of guests was not seated at its assigned time. When the guests arrived, an explanation was offered to them, admitting that it was the restaurant's problem, not theirs.

Taking reservations and blocking requires a lot of organisation and pre-planning, but it allows the restaurant to have a table ready for the guest and to avoid overbooking. Some would say it is too much work to do all that pre-planning. Some would say, "I'll take some short-cuts and not put the names next to the table." This can be done if the host is experienced and knows the room. But it comes only with time and experience. A person using this system initially should follow the steps stated above, and the problems of overbooking will be eliminated.

Many guests will not patronize a restaurant that does not take reservations. Long waits for a table prompt many complaints from guests. Restaurants have a relatively new technique called call-ahead or priority seating. Guests call the restaurant and have their name added to the seating list. It holds a waiting spot for the guest for dinner that day. The guest's name is logged immediately onto the seating list so that when he or she arrives, the wait will not be as long. It does not guarantee the guest a table for a certain time, but a place in line. The guest is waiting some other place than in the restaurant; therefore, this system keeps the wait to a minimum.

A major problem that restaurants have in taking reservations is with guests who do not show up for their reservations. Restaurants have been trying to solve the problem of no-shows for many years. There are some proven methods that work in reducing the number of no-shows. The first step in preventing no-shows is to properly train the person who takes reservations. Proper training means informing the guest of all, policies of the restaurant pertaining to the reservation. Also, when the guest makes a reservation, information has to be obtained correctly.

Some restaurants request the guest to call them back on the day of the reservation to confirm the reservation.

The guests are told that if they are unable to be reached, their reservation will not be honoured unless the guests themselves confirm the reservation. Other restaurants have begun to employ the same methods as hotels do for lodging rooms: they take a deposit for the reservations. In towns where there is a large demand for tables on weekends, restaurants have asked for a guest's credit card number or for cash to hold the table. Some owners use a personal computer to keep track of guests who are no-shows. Once the guest becomes a no-show, the name is put on an alphabetised list for the reservation taker.

When a guest calls and asks for a reservation, the name is checked against the list. If the name is on the list, the employee informs the guest that there was a reservation scheduled for a certain date for which the guest did not show up. The policy is further explained to the guest that if he or she does not show up for the reservation or does not cancel, then the restaurant will no longer take any reservations under his or her name. By using one or a combination of these methods, the number of noshows in the restaurant will be greatly decreased.

12

TABLE MANNERS

No surer gauge of the native refinement of any person can be, found than the manners which they show at the table. It is incumbent upon parents to train their children in those niceties of etiquette which will grow with their growth, and make their progress through life far easier.

Who does not feel compassion for that young person who is, at the very outset of his career, confronted with the dread lest he make an exhibition of his lack of good manners? By commencing to instill simple forms of good-breeding into the child in its earliest years, they become habitual, and their performance a second nature.

CHILDREN SHOULD BE INSTRUCTED

Children should be early, brought to the table, that they may' benefit by association with those whose manners are fixed. By such association they will acquire an ease and readiness which will serve them well when they in turn become entertainers, in their after life.

POLITENESS

The enjoyment of the family meal is greatly enhanced when each member is polite and attentive to the others;

when parents and children alike are cheerful, agreeable and look after each other's comfort.

Children Allowed to Talk at Table

The children in a, household should be encouraged to talk, but not permitted to show off, and say smart things. There is a great temptation on the part of fond parents to tell the bright sayings and doings of their offspring to strangers, in their presence; this should never be indulged in, as it not alone makes the little one have an undue idea of its own importance, but it becomes annoying to strangers, who, although they may be very partial to a bright child, do not want to hear its praises sounded continually.

Manners of the Little Ones

Children should wait quietly, until their elders are served.. This will be difficult for them no doubt, for nearly all children are gifted with healthy appetites, but if the habit of waiting is enforced, it will become easy to them.

Loud Talking Prohibited

Loud talking on their part should be prohibited, as also interrupting conversation. They should not whisper, however, or glance around the table and giggle. Neither should an older child reprove the wee ones aloud for any breach of good manners, or direct the attention of the mother to it in the presence of others. A look, or low-spoken word will remind the offending one and save it mortification.

When Children Leave the Table

If children are compelled to leave the table before the rest of the family, so as to reach school, they should rise quietly, ask to be excused and leave the apartment so as not to disturb anyone.

Do Not Let them Eat Greedily

They should not eat greedily, cramming their mouths full, nor smack their lips, tilt their chairs back, or drop their knives carelessly on the table-cloth. The knife and fork should be laid across the plate, with the handles to the right, when the meal is finished.

Grown People at Fault

While children's manners are thus alluded to, we regret to say that they are not the sole violators of good-breeding. To any one who observes much, it is astonishing that so many well-dressed people, who seem to know so much, are so shockingly rude at the table. Such people are sometimes guilty of acts which are revolting. The well-bred will always regard the prejudices of those around them, and try not to offend in any manner.

Begging Compliments

Don't solicit compliments for your food, by laying stress upon the care with which it is prepared. If it is good, the guest will not be slow in complimenting you, although this should be done without approaching to flattery. It would be a great shock to one's self-love if some blunt, ill-bred guest should agree with you when you declared that such and such a dish was scarcely worth eating. You were sorry that you had no better to offer. Say nothing about the food you set before your guests; but by its abundance and the welcome you give him, will he measure its value.

Refusing an Article of Food

If a guest does not care for a certain article on the table, or for some reason does not wish to partake of it, he should not refuse it by stating that "Cheese don't agree with me," or "I can't endure tomatoes," but simply say – "I do not care for any, thank you." We well remember the horror and disgust with which an apparently well-bred lady filled her listeners at the table by declining a certain dish with the assertion that "It took too long to digest, and her doctor had forbidden it."

Rudeness at Table

There are many little rudenesses which can be avoided at the table, and which a little thought would instinctively pronounce offensive. Among these are coughing or breathing into your neighbour's face. Fidgeting in your seat, or moving about restlessly; drumming upon the table with your fingers; whispering confidentially with your neighbour; emphasizing your remarks by flourishing your fork, to the risk of your neighbour's eyes; leaning the elbows upon the table; standing up and reaching across the table in place of requesting that what you want be passed you. All these acts of ill-breeding or thoughtlessness we have seen perpetrated by those who should know better.

Things to Avoid

— Do not eat onions or garlic before going into company. They may be very healthy, but they are -also very offensive.

— Do not talk loudly or boisterously., but be cheerful and companionable, not monopolizing the conversation, but joining in it. Never butter a slice of bread and bite into it like a hungry school-boy, and do not cut the slice into halves or quarters with your knife, but break off a piece, when wanted, and then butter and eat it. Do not break the bread into your soup.

— As in serving the courses, each plate, with a knife and fork upon it, is set before you, remove the knife and fork instantly, and lay them beside the plate. To neglect this will force the servants to remove them, and delay' the progress of the dinner.

— Do not twirl a goblet, or rattle the knife and fork, or show anything which will look like impatience or eagerness to commence the meal.

— Bones and fragments should be deposited on the edge of your plate, so as not to soil the table-cloth. If you by accident spill coffee or tea, do not apologize. It is understood that you did not do it intentionally. The servant should at once spread a clean napkin over the stain.

— Never turn tea or coffee into your saucer to cool it. If you wish a second cup, place the spoon in the saucer before passing it to be refilled. Do not stand a dripping cup on the table-cloth. Never blow soup to make it cool.

— It is very rude to pick your teeth at the table after a meal is completed.

— Napkins are to wipe the mouth with, not to mop the forehead or nose.

— Never put your own knife, fork or spoon into a dish from which others are to be helped.

Dress for the Occasion

The table being a meeting place where everything should

be nice and conducive to good manners, a gentleman will never appear at it in his shirt sleeves. If it is excessively warm weather, and he wishes to enjoy the freedom of his own home table, he can don a light coat of seersucker, farmer's satin, or similar material; but in public he will always retain the coat which he wears through the day, save of course, on dress occasions, of which we have spoken elsewhere.

A lady should observe the same care in her dress. Untidy hair and dirty nails are especially repellant.

Serving at Table

- The one who serves at table, should not help too abundantly, or flood food with gravies. Many do not like them; and it is better to allow each guest to help himself. Water is poured at the right of a guest – everything else is passed from the left.
- Do not watch the dishes as they are uncovered. Or talk with the mouth full.
- If you discover something objectionable in the food do not attract the attention of others to it, but quietly deposit it under the edge of your plate.

Do not Sop Gravy etc.

- Never sop up your gravy or preserves with bread, And do not scrape your plate so as to obtain the last bit, or drink as though you were dying of thirst. It is quite an art to drink gracefully. Don't throw your head back and raise the glass perpendicularly, but carry the glass to your lips, and by lifting it to a slight angle, you easily drain its contents.
- Be careful not to stretch your feet across the room, under the table. It is very disagreeable to be kicked, even accidentally.

— In leaving the table, if business or an engagement compels you to, excuse yourself. It is only in hotels or boarding-houses that this is permitted to pass unnoticed.

— It is rude to handle the bread or cake which is offered you. Only touch the piece which you intend to eat.

Eat What you Wish at the Table

— Never carry fruit or confectionery away from the table. Eat what you wish while there.

"There is difference of opinion as to who should be first served at table, many insisting that the old fashion of serving the hostess first should be continued; but as this originated in the days when people were in the habit of poisoning guests by the wholesale, as a convenient way of ridding themselves and the world of them, there seems to be no reason why it should be observed now. Then guests preferred that the hostess should show her confidence in the viands set before them, before partaking themselves; but the natural instincts of propriety seem to indicate that the most honored guest, that is, the lady at the right of the host, should be first served."

— Whom a Gentleman Should Serve

— A gentleman seated by a lady or an elderly person passes the water or whatever may be required by his neighbour at the table.

Do not Read the Table

— Never bring a book or paper to the table to read. It is allowable at a hotel or restaurant, where you are not anxious to form promiscuous acquaintances, but among friends, the gaps should be filled in by cheerful and enlivening conversation.

— Remove fish bones before eating, but should one get into the mouth, remove it by placing the napkin before the mouth.

— Everything that it is possible to cut or break with a fork should be eaten without a knife.

Objecting to Wine

— Should you have scruples about taking wine at the dinner table, it is not necessary to enter into an explanation of them, and thus bring around your unfortunate head a veritable "hornet's nest" of ridicule and argument from unthinking people. Merely decline it, in a quiet and respectful manner. Those whose opinion is worth having, will see nothing singular in the fact that you do not use wine.

— Eat slowly, as a measure of health, as well as manners.

Make your Plate Palatable-Looking

Do not mix your food on your plate with the knife. It looks as though you set no score by the nice care with which the various articles had been prepared. It were all the same to you, whether it were fish or fowl – it was only made to be devoured, not eaten.

Paring fruit

Never pare fruit for a lady, unless asked to do so, and then hold it upon the fork which belongs to her. Apples should be pared with silver fruit knives, and quartered and each slice carried to the mouth on the point of the knife. Still, there are many well-bred people who only enjoy apples when they can eat them as they did in their childhood's days, without the aid of a knife or fork.

Chinese Table Manners

The main difference between Chinese and western eating habits is that unlike the West, where everyone has their own plate of food, in China the dishes are placed on the table and everybody shares. If you are being treated by a Chinese host, be prepared for a ton of food. Chinese are very proud of their culture of cuisine and will do their best to show their hospitality. And sometimes the Chinese host use their chopsticks to put food in your bowl or plate. This is a sign of politeness. The appropriate thing to do would be to eat the whatever-it-is and say how yummy it is. If you feel uncomfortable with this, you can just say a polite thank you and leave the food there.

Eating No-no's

Don't stick your chopsticks upright in the rice bowl.Instead,lay them on your dish. The reason for this is that when somebody dies,the shrine to them contains a bowl of sand or rice with two sticks of incense stuck upright in it. So if you stick your chopsticks in the rice bowl, it looks like this shrine and is equivalent to wishing death upon a person at the table!

Make sure the spout of the teapot is not facing anyone. It is impolite to set the teapot down where the spout is facing towards somebody. The spout should always be directed to where nobody is sitting, usually just outward from the table.

Don't tap on your bowl with your chopsticks.Beggars tap on their bowls, so this is not polite.Also, when the food is coming too slow in a restarant, people will tap their bowls. If you are in someone's home,it is like insulting the cook.

Drinking

Besides beer, the official Chinese alcoholic beverage is Bai Jiu,high-proof Chinese liquor made from assorted grains. There are varying degrees of Bai Jiu. The Beijing favorite is called Er Guo Tou, which is a whopping 56% alcohol. More expensive are Maotai and Wuliangye.

American Table Manners

Manners aside, all was not well at the American table. Numerous commentators noted the absence of the husband from the domestic table, American's refusal to carry on friendly conversation while eating, and a tendency to eat rapidly and get the job of eating over as soon as possible. It was little wonder that dyspepsia (indigestion) was considered an epidemic among American men.

Rules

— Do not play with the table utensils or crumble the bread.

— Do not put your elbows on the table, or sit too far back, or lounge

— Do not talk loud or boisterously

— Be cheerful in conduct or conversation

— Never, if possible, cough or sneeze at the table.

— Never tilt back your chair while at the table, or at any other time.

— Do not talk when the mouth is full

— Never make a noise while eating

— Do not open the mouth while chewing, but keep the lips closed. It is not necessary to show people how you masticate your food.

— Never indicate that you notice anything unpleasant in the food.

— Do not break your bread into the soup, nor mix with gravy. It is bad taste to mix food on the plate.

— Never leave the table before the rest of the family or guests, without asking the host or hostess to excuse you.

— Eat soup with the side of the spoon, without noise.

— The fork is used to convey the food to the mouth, except when a spoon is necessary for liquids.

— Raw oysters are eaten with a fork.

— If you wish to be served with more tea or coffee, place your spoon in your saucer.

— Tea or coffee should never be poured into the saucer to cool, but sipped from the cup.

— If a dish is presented to you, serve yourself first and then pass it on.

— Never allow butter, soup or other food to remain on your whiskers

— Never wear gloves at the table, unless your hands are for some special reason unfit to be seen.

— Never, when serving others, overload the plate nor force upon them delicacies which they decline.

— Never make a great display when removing hair, insects or other disagreeable things from your food. Place them quietly under the edge of your plate.

— Eat Cheese with a fork, not a knife

— Ask a servant in a low tone for what you want

— Break your bread, do not cut it.

— Eat fruit with silver knives and forks

— If you prefer, take up asparagus with the fingers. Olives and artichokes are always so eaten

— If a course is set before you that you do not wish, do not touch it.

— It is not your business to reprove the waiter for improper conduct; that belongs to your host.

— A gentleman must help a lady whom he has escorted to the table, to all she wishes; but it is improper for him to offer to help other ladies who have escorts

— Use a napkin only for your mouth. Never use it for your nose, face or forehead.

— It is very rude to pick your teeth at the table. If it becomes necessary to do so, hold your napkin over your mouth.

There is not much call for a complete working knowledge of table manners in America today. Many families only gather all at once around the dinner table at holiday feasts, and most restaurants are too casual to require, or even to allow for, more than basic good table manners. If, having dropped his napkin, a diner at a bistro were to attempt to practice proper etiquette by signaling a member of the staff to bring a fresh one, he would probably have to do without a napkin at all. Try as he might to make eye contact and indicate the nature of the problem with a subtle wiggle of the eyebrow and downward flicker of the glance, he is likely to succeed only in causing his date to think he is making a play for the server. Although strict good manners forbid placing a used eating utensil back on the table, the server removing a plate on which a fork has quite properly been positioned "pointing at 11 o'clock" might just plop that item back where it started, making more of a clatter than if the diner had simply done it herself.

From time to time—perhaps at an important business dinner, a romantic date at an expensive restaurant, or a first dinner with the family of the person who may be "the One"—it is necessary to display a more sophisticated knowledge of table etiquette. This is not difficult, once you have mastered the basics. Anyone armed with this core knowledge and the ability to adapt smoothly to the situation at hand will be able to handle even the most formal event. The goal is not, after all, to demonstrate utter mastery of the most arcane details of etiquette (which would be quite difficult considering the wide variations of customs in different cultures and from generation to generation), but rather to behave with graciousness and poise at the table.

Indians have notoriously poor table manners. We slurp our soup, chomp our chocolate cake, spill our salt, and belch our blessings. And while all this slurping, chomping, spilling, and belching can be seen as quaintly charming, we are no longer living in little wooden shacks in the Ozarks where we prop our feet on the table and scoot aside to make room for our 26 cats, dogs, and other varmints. We're not going to teach you about lesser-used table items (such as fingerbowls) because frankly, you almost never use those things, and even when you do, no one else will know how to use them either.

Secret of the Formal Place Setting

There is a general consensus among writers of etiquette manuals that too many people are afraid they will fail to choose the proper utensil for the appropriate stage of the meal. Book after book provides reassurance on this point: use the outermost utensil or utensils, as necessary, one set for each course, and you can't go wrong (unless the table has been improperly laid to start out with).

For a formal place setting, you will receive exactly as much silverware as you will need, arranged in precisely the right order. Good etiquette requires you to assume (and this ought to ease most people's worries) that the host has correctly assigned each utensil to its task, rather than attempt to point out that a fish fork is improperly being supplied for your salad. As each course is finished, the silverware will be removed with the dish, leaving you with a clean slate, all ready for the next item to arrive. Common sense forbids arranging battalions of forks and knives at the sides of the plate, so on the extremely rare occasions that more than three or four courses are planned, new silverware will be brought to you after all of the original setting has been used.

The plate in this setting is known as a "service plate," and is never actually eaten from. It will either be removed when the first course is brought, or the dish will be set on top of it. A person faced with this array can expect to dine on:

Oysters, as Appetizer

Use the small fork angled into the soupspoon at right. This is the one exception to the rule of placing forks to the left of the plate.

Soup

The soupspoon is commonly the only spoon provided for the initial place setting.

Salad

Note the thicker tine at the left of the fork, which strengthens the tool—for right handed people—for use in cutting large salad greens without having to resort to the knife.

Fish

Both a fork and a knife are provided for fish. Sometimes

the fish knife has a silver blade, because fish, which is often served with lemon, reacts with the steel in old knife blades, causing an unpleasant taste (the invention of stainless steel in the 1920s made this problem obsolete). The fish fork is usually shorter than the meat fork.

Meat

The inner fork and knife are provided for the meat course of the meal.

Dessert

In this case, the dessert utensils will be brought in with the dessert. However, you may encounter the dessert spoon—and fork, if needed—as part of the initial place setting. They would be placed horizontally over the plate and parallel to each other, with the bowl of the spoon pointing to the left and the tines of the fork pointing right. When coffee and tea are served, a teaspoon will be provided; it is brought in on the saucer.

There are so many rules about proper table manners that it would take forever to list every nitpicky item. So let's move right to the meal. But wait! Should a man pull a woman's chair out for her before she sits? Well, it depends. If they are on a date in a nice restaurant, sure. But at a nice restaurant, the person who seats the couple will probably pull the chair out for her, so you have nothing to worry about. This leads to...

Tip - 1: For all questions involving etiquette, just use your brains

Men don't have to get all Victorian and insist on standing up every time a woman leaves or returns to the table. Just be polite. Now, if you're a guest at someone's house, don't sit until the host sits first (unless the host told you to just go sit down at the table). In fact, when dealing with hosts, remember...

Tip - 2: Never do anything until the host does it first

This includes sit, eat, put your napkin on the table, and leave. After all, the host is paying for the shindig, so at least make him/her feel like (s)he's in charge.

OK, so we've overcome the enormous hurdle of getting your rump into the chair. Now it's time to take inventory and figure out which stuff is yours. We've all gone to a dinner and used our neighbour's fork, glass, bread plate, or husband. My, how embarrassing! So here's a shortcut so that you can know exactly what is yours: (1) Your plate is in the center. (2) Knives and spoons are on your right, and forks and your napkin on the left. (3) Liquids (e.g., your water) go to your right, and solids (e.g., bread plate) go on your left. Here's a funky example of what the utensil layout in front of you may look like:

There might be more forks, knives, or spoons, depending on what the meal is, but you get the general idea. If you need another shortcut, remember that your drink is always on the right because the first two letters in the word "DRink" stand for "Drink Right." Catchy, eh? Just know that your bread plate is on the other side, and you're set!

One note if you happen to be the host: remember that all items (e.g., salad, meal, wine, water) should be brought to each diner's RIGHT, and cleared from each diner's LEFT. That's why the glasses are all on the right.

There are so many rules about proper table manners that it would take forever to list every nitpicky item. So let's move right to the meal. But wait! Should a man pull a woman's chair out for her before she sits? Well, it depends. If they are on a date in a nice restaurant, sure.

But at a nice restaurant, the person who seats the couple will probably pull the chair out for her, so you have nothing to worry about.

OK, hot shot. You know where your stuff is. But now it's time to know how to use everything properly. Take your napkin and place it in your lap right away when you sit down. (It should never be on the table.) Don't get fancy and try to snap it open. Just put it on your lap (NOT into your shirt). If you're a man, do not put your tie over your shoulder.

Now you can take some bread from the breadbasket. Take only one slice of bread. (It's OK to rip it from the loaf with your hands, but be neat. Don't declare war on the bread and cheer when you get your slice separated.) Here's a common mistake: DO NOT butter your bread at this point. Yeah, you heard us. This is how to do it:

1. Take some butter, and put it on your plate, not on the bread. Now you have your own little pile of butter and won't continually fish from the communal butter dish.
2. Tear a bite-size piece off of your bread.
3. Butter that bite-sized piece from your own little butter pile.
4. Eat it with delight.

The first part of the meal comes: the appetizers. But what utensil should you use?

Tip 3: Use your utensils from the outside in

The fork furthest to the outside is the one you should use for the appetizer. When the next part of the meal comes, use the next outermost fork, and so on. Same deal goes for the spoons and knives. If you're in a fancy restaurant or a party at Buckingham Palace, you might be lucky enough to have waiters who will remove any utensils you won't need. But even if you do not have this luxury, we still implore: use your brains! You won't use a knife to eat your soup. You won't use a spoon to eat your salad. But let's say that you lose track of your utensils and get lost. Then, proceed to...

Tip - 4: If you're not sure what to do, wait and see what your neighbour does. If that offers no clue, then just fake it

Chances are, nobody's watching you closely enough to see that you're using your dinner fork instead of the salad fork (the salad fork is the smaller one). Don't draw attention to yourself. Don't make a big deal of it. Just take a guess and eat. If you used the wrong utensil, the waiter will bring you a replacement.

Here is the proper technique for using a fork and knife. Assuming you are right-handed, hold the fork in your left hand and knife in your right. With the tines facing downward (curving towards you), hold down an end-piece of whatever you are cutting (let's assume it's meat). Do not hold the knife or fork like a dagger, but rather, place your index finger along the top of each utensil, holding each at the end. This gives you greater control without looking like you're hacking into the poor dead animal.

Gently, using a sawing motion, cut the meat near the tines of the fork, so that you have one bite-sized piece. Then, lay the knife down (without allowing it to touch the table), and switch the fork (complete with pierced meat) to your right hand. Bring it up to your mouth, chew quietly, and swallow when the meat is sufficiently masticated. This is called the American (or Zig-Zag) method of cutting food. The Continental (or European) method consists of not switching hands, and using the left hand for all fork-related activities.

Before we move on, remember the thing we said about not letting the knife touch the table?

Tip - 5: You should never let any utensils, once used, EVER touch the table again

This includes leaning a fork onto the plate, or using a knife and putting it back in its original place. The original reason is because the utensil could dirty the tablecloth (a major faux pas) and result in a cleaning bill for the host. So once a utensil is used, it's lifespan is over. Get over it, and leave it on the plate at all times.

One last note should be made about soup. Many people do not know how to correctly use a soup spoon, so we will supply you with...

Tip - 6: Do not put the entire soup spoon in your mouth

Instead, fill a soup spoon about 75% with soup, bring it up to your mouth, and sip it from the side with as little slurping as possible. When your soup runs low, it's acceptable to tip your bowl away from you so that you can capture the last bits of soup, but don't do that more than twice. And remember to lower your spoon into your soup gently so that it doesn't bang the bottom of the bowl. Imagine 20 people eating soup and banging their bowl bottoms.

Tip - 7: If you spill something, don't make a big deal of it

It happens. Just be calm, quietly apologize, try to prevent anything from spilling over onto the people sitting next to you with your napkin, and get a waiter to help you control the damage. If something spills onto someone's clothes, do NOT try to get it off his or her clothes. That's technically known as a "sexual harassment lawsuit waiting to happen." Point it out, let them clean it up, offer to pay the dry cleaning bill, and then let it go. Hey, as we all learned when we were two years old, accidents happen, and they can often be wet and messy. Just keep your cool. Oh, and if your pet monkey poops on the table, then carefully remove the primate, and take everyone out to a very expensive restaurant where monkey brains are on the menu.

A big question regarding eating properly is when it's OK to use your fingers, and when you must use a utensil. While we provide a small list of finger foods, there is a tip you can follow.

Tip - 8: If you're not sure whether or not you can eat something with your fingers, just use a utensil

Hey, we're not brain surgeons here, but this just makes sense. Better to be over-careful than under-careful. As for foods that you can eat with your fingers, they include:

— artichoke

— asparagus (as long as there is no goo on it, and it's not too long)

— bacon (but only if it is crisp)

— sandwiches

— cookies

— small fruits or berries with stems

— french fries and potato chips

— hamburgers and hot dogs

— corn on the cob

— caviar

— pickles

Pacing

This is not the Indy 500, and the food is not going to walk away. So take your time! Don't fill your mouth with too much food. Try to keep the same eating pace as your host, so that you all finish at the same time. It is not a compliment when someone leans over and says "Boy, good thing you didn't eat the plate" or "Wanna finish some time before the next thaw?"

Mom-isms

Just think of this as the potpourri of things you've heard all your life about table manners. Most of them were 100% correct:

— don't grab food
— don't talk with your mouth full
— chew with your mouth closed and no noise
— excuse yourself if you get up to go somewhere (e.g., bathroom, to make a call)
— don't pick something out of your teeth (just excuse yourself to the bathroom)
— don't leave lipstick smears on anything
— don't put crap on the table (meaning a purse, papers, keys, or monkey poop)
— don't smoke
— don't tilt or squirm in your chair

How to Use Utensils

The rules that specify how knife, fork, and spoon must be used have evolved along with the forms of the utensils themselves. In general, these rules are explicitly intended to prevent the utensils from appearing threatening.

Margaret Visser, in her book The Rituals of Dinner, points out that etiquette and the ritual it imposes helps to control the violence inherent in the preparation and serving of meals.

Animals are slaughtered and consumed, the guest-host relationship is, in itself, a complicated interweaving of the imposition of obligation and suspension of hostility, and the ordinary table knife is related to actual weapons of war. Consequently, flatware is held delicately, carefully balanced on the prescribed fingers and guided by the fingertips. To hold any utensil in a fist or to manipulate it in such a way that is pointed at anyone would hint at potential danger, as would even setting it down in an inappropriate way.

Holding a Utensil

In general use, both spoon and fork are held horizontally by balancing them between the first knuckle of the middle finger and the tip of the index finger while the thumb steadies the handle. The knife is used with the tip of the index finger gently pressing out over the top of the blade to guide as you cut.

The Zig Zag Method

By American custom, which was brought about partly by the late introduction of the fork into the culture, all three utensils are intended for use primarily with the right hand, which is the more capable hand for most people. This leads to some complicated maneuvering when foods, such as meat, require the use of knife and fork to obtain a bite of manageable size. When this is the case, the fork is held in the left hand, turned so that the tines point downward, the better to hold the meat in place while the right hand operates the knife. After a bite-sized piece has been cut, the diner sets the knife down on the plate and transfers the fork to the right hand, so that it can be used to carry the newly cut morsel to the mouth. Emily Post calls this the "zig-zag" style.

European Style

The European, or "Continental," style of using knife and fork is somewhat more efficient, and its practice is also common in the United States, where left-handed children are no longer forced to learn to wield a fork with their right hands. According to this method, the fork is held continuously in the left hand and used for eating. When food must be cut, the fork is used exactly as in the American style, except that once the bite has been separated from the whole, it is conveyed directly to the mouth on the downward-facing fork. Regardless of which style is used to operate fork and knife, it is important never to cut more than one or two bites at one time.

Peas

Another significant difference between the American and the Continental styles of using knife and fork is the American insistence that even the most awkward and contrary foods (peas being the traditional example) must be captured by the unaided fork. In Europe it is permitted to use the knife or a small bit of bread to ease a stubborn item onto the fork.

Placement

There are numerous rules and prohibitions regarding the proper placement of eating utensils once they have been used. Essentially, used flatware must never be allowed to touch the surface of the table, where it might dirty the cloth. It is not proper to allow even the clean handle of a knife or fork to rest on the cloth while the other end lies on the plate. At the end of a course, a utensil must not be left in any dish that is not flat—the soup bowl, for example, or a shrimp cocktail dish, a teacup or a parfait glass. All these items are usually presented with a plate underneath the bowl or cup, on which the utensil must be placed after use.

The positioning of knife and fork when not in use acts as a sort of semaphore, allowing the diner to indicate the degree to which he intends to pause in eating. Flatware should always be placed on the plate during pauses between bites. If this is to be a very short time, there is no set pattern. For longer waits, perhaps caused by a diverting twist in the table conversation, the diner places the fork on the left and knife on the right, so that they cross over the center of the plate. The diner preparing to pass his plate for a second helping places the fork and knife parallel to each other at the right side of the plate, so that there is room for the food. When the diner has finished, he signals this by setting the fork and knife parallel to each other, so they lie either horizontally across the center of the plate or are on the diagonal, with the handles pointing to the right. The cutting edge of the knife blade should face toward the diner (again, avoiding all possible aggressive implications), and the fork may be placed with the tines either up or down.

How to Use a Napkin

Using the napkin at formal occasions, as with much else associated with etiquette, should be a delicate affair. It is meant only to be dabbed at the lips and should not get dirty in the process. It might seem that the napkin is provided precisely so that it can help the diner clean up any mess that might occur during the course of the meal. Of course, this was its original use, (once the tablecloth itself ceased to be used as a napkin), and at an informal occasion such as a barbeque, it still performs this service. But the more formal the event, the more vestigial the presence of the napkin, because the purpose of nearly every aspect of table manners is to preserve cleanliness and proper appearance. If all other elements of the meal are going well, there will be no danger of smudging the linen.

As soon as you are seated, remove the napkin from your place setting, unfold it, and put it in your lap. At some very formal restaurants, the waiter may do this for the diners, but it is not inappropriate to place your own napkin in your lap, even when this is the case. If your napkin falls on the floor during a very formal event, do not retrieve it. You should be able to signal a member of the serving staff that you need a fresh one.

When you leave the table at the end of the meal, place your napkin loosely next to your plate. It should not be crumpled or twisted, which would reveal untidiness or nervousness, respectively; nor should it be folded, which might be seen as an implication that you think your hosts might reuse it without washing. The napkin must also not be left on the chair. There is a European superstition that a diner who leaves the napkin on his chair will never sit at that table again, but other, less supernatural, reasons are often cited for this: it might seem as if you have an inappropriately dirty napkin to hide—or even that you are trying to run off with the table linens.

So now you are sitting at a lovely dinner, using your eating utensils in the most proper way possible. And then you let an enormous burp fly. Whoops! There are a lot more to table manners than just using the right fork. You also have to have correct manners with regard to how you eat.

Posture

Always sit straight up in your chair, never leaning backward, nor forward. Never let your elbows touch the table (though you can put your hands on the table all you want). When eating, do not bring your face toward the plate (a la a pig's trough), but bring the utensil up to you. You're the master! But what if you drop something? You should suavely signal a waiter so that (s)he could replace the item. But if it's your napkin that escaped, just excuse yourself as you lean down, pick it up, and continue with whatever you were doing.

Passing Stuff

If someone asks for something to be passed to him or her, only reach for it if you are the closest one to the item. In that case, take the one item and place it directly next to your neighbour. (Do not pass it hand-to-hand.) Continue passing the item in this manner until the original requester has the item. And oddly enough, you are not allowed to help yourself to the item until the original requester gets a chance at it (after all, (s)he asked first). When that person is done, you can ask the item to be passed back to you, and enjoy!

Salt and Pepper

An additional note needs to be made about using salt and pepper: if someone asks you to pass the salt, do it in the same manner above, but pass both the salt and pepper (even if only one of the two were asked for). Again, do not use guerrilla tactics and try to use the salt until after the original requester had a chance with it. Also, never use salt or pepper on your food until after you have already tasted it. It's a huge insult to the cook if you try to add flavor before even tasting it stag. And while we think it's blatantly obvious, we'd feel guilty if we didn't remind you: don't ever season a dish that everyone is supposed to share (not with salt, pepper, catsup, parmesan cheese, not with anything). Keep your own creative additions to your own plate.

"Embarrassing" Moments

Did you burp? Did you spill something? Did your pet monkey poop on the table? To handle these little unfortunate accidents, just try to channel the aura of James Bond and think: be classy, be classy, be classy. If anything comes out of your mouth other than speech (e.g., burp, hiccup, chicken nugget), just excuse yourself quietly (to nobody in particular), and put your napkin to your lips. This is a good time to talk about general napkin etiquette. Never smear your napkin all over your face, or wipe your mouth hard. Just use it to blot your mouth. But if you spill something, then follow...

Tips and Pitfalls

Beginning

Developing the habit of taking a moment to observe which starting method will be operative at an event can be very useful in preventing awkward mistakes. It will ensure, for example, that an agnostic guest never finds himself with laden fork pushed halfway into his mouth just as the host begins to say grace.

There are two common approaches to determining how to begin, and, whichever method is used, it should be followed at the start of each course of the meal. At smaller events, it is common to wait to take a bite until everyone at the table has received a serving and the hostess has begun eating. Sometimes a hostess may urge her guests to eat immediately upon receiving the food. This is especially true at larger events, where waiting for everyone would allow it to get cold. In this case, wait until one or two of the other guests are ready to begin as well, so that you are not the only person at the table who is eating.

Posture

Proper posture at the table is very important. Sit up straight, with your arms held near your body. You should neither lean on the back of the chair nor bend forward to place the elbows on the table. It is permissible to lean forward slightly every now and then and press the elbows very lightly against the edge of the table, if it is obvious that you are not using them for support.

Eating soup

Dip the spoon into the soup, moving it away from the body, until it is about two-thirds full, then sip the liquid (without slurping) from the side of the spoon (without inserting the whole bowl of the spoon into the mouth). The theory behind this is that a diner who scoops the spoon toward himself is more likely to slosh soup onto his lap, although it is difficult to imagine what sort of eater would stroke the spoon so forcefully through the liquid that he creates waves. It is perfectly fine to tilt the bowl slightly—again away from the body—to get the last spoonful or two of soup.

Eating bouillon

It is not very well known, undoubtedly because it is no longer in fashion to serve it, that if you are given bouillon in a soup cup with a handle, you may pick up the cup and sip the broth directly from it, even if a soupspoon has been provided. If there are any bits of vegetables or meat in the bouillon, they should be eaten with the spoon before you begin sipping.

Finger bowls

The finger bowl has hovered on the brink of obsolescence for over a century without entirely disappearing. This is probably why it provides the critical obstacle in the story of the man, either a foreigner or a bumpkin (depending on the teller), who is a guest at a formal dinner party. When a servant offers him a bowl of water at the end of the meal, he drinks it. The hostess presiding at the event is so poised and utterly well-mannered that, without skipping a beat, she drinks her bowl down, too, thus saving him the embarrassment of realizing the extent of his faux pas. This tale has reached almost the status of urban legend, and it is told in many variations. The hostess may be a family matriarch or someone very well-known, say Eleanor Roosevelt or Queen Victoria, but the finger bowl seems to be a constant.

Fortunately, the main difficulty lies in recognizing the finger bowl when you see it, which, at formal events, will be either before or after the dessert course. Often there is a slice of lemon floating in the water. Once you are presented with one, all you need to know is that you should delicately dip your fingertips in the water (no scrubbing), dry them off with your napkin (equally delicately), and set the bowl to the side of your plate.

Offering food

Take note, when you are the host of a party, of the way you offer additional servings to your guests. Urging someone to "have another (or a second or third) helping" can be seen as an unpleasant insinuation that the guest has eaten too much. It is best to phrase each offer of food as if the dish has just been brought out for the first time.

Pass the salt

The proper response to this very simple sounding request is to pick up both the salt and the pepper and to place them on the table within reach of the person next to you, who will do the same, and so on, until they reach the person who asked for them. They are not passed hand-to-hand, nor should anyone other than the original requester sprinkle her food when she has the shakers in her possession. The reason for this, as Judith Martin points out more than once, is that American etiquette is not about efficiency. Often, the most refined action is that which requires the greatest number of steps to carry it out.

Removing inedible items from the mouth

The general rule for removing food from your mouth is that it should go out the same way it went in. Therefore, olive pits can be delicately dropped onto an open palm before putting them onto your plate, and a piece of bone discovered in a bite of chicken should be returned to the plate by way of the fork. Fish is an exception to the rule. It is fine to remove the tiny bones with your fingers, since they would be difficult to drop from your mouth onto the fork. And, of course, if what you have to spit out will be terrifically ugly—an extremely fatty piece of meat that you simply can't bring yourself to swallow, for example—it will be necessary to surreptitiously spit it into your napkin, so that you can keep it out of sight.

Eat with Your Fingers

Artichoke

The artichoke is actually the leaf-enclosed flower bud of a

plant that is in the thistle family. It is usually served steamed with a dipping sauce. To eat it, pull a leaf off, dip it, scrape the flesh from the base of the leaf with your top teeth, and discard the leaf on the plate provided for that purpose. Continue eating the leaves until the prickly "choke" is revealed—this is the point when it is clear you have a species of thistle in front of you. Switch to fork and knife, first to remove the choke, then to eat the heart and base.

Asparagus

Asparagus may be eaten with the fingers as long as it is not covered with sauce or otherwise prepared so it is too mushy to pick up easily. Of course, it is also just fine to use a fork and knife to eat asparagus, even when it is perfectly al dente and sauce-free. But you might appreciate getting to act like a rebel without breaking any rules.

Bacon

When bacon is cooked until it is very crisp, and there is no danger of getting the fingers wet with grease, it is okay to pick it up to eat it. This is an instance of practicality winning out over decorum, since trying to cut a crisp piece of bacon usually results in crushing it into shards that are quite difficult to round up onto a fork.

Bread

Bread must always be broken, never cut with a knife. Tear off a piece that is no bigger than two bites worth and eat that before tearing off another. If butter is provided (and at formal events it customarily is not), butter the small piece just before eating it. There is an exception to this rule: if you are served a hot roll, it is permissible to tear (not cut) the whole roll lengthwise down the middle and place a pat of butter inside to melt.

Cookies

It is never necessary to try to eat the cookie that comes as a garnish to your dessert with a spoon. Unless it has fallen so far into the chocolate sauce that there isn't a clean corner by which to pick it up.

Corn on the Cob

It is unlikely that it will be served at a formal event, but if you encounter corn on the cob, it may be picked up and eaten. The approved method of doing so is to butter one or two rows at a time and to eat across the cob cleanly.

Chips, french fries, fried chicken, and hamburgers

All these items (which could also probably be classified as "fast foods") simply will not be served in a formal setting. Most are intended to be eaten with the hands, although a particularly messy hamburger could be approached with fork and knife, and steak fries (the thick-cut, less crispy variety) may be best eaten with a fork.

Almost everything that is served at a cocktail party or during a pre-meal cocktail hour is intended to be eaten with the fingers. Some of these foods make appearances at regular meals as well (although not often very formal ones). When they do, it is still permissible to use the fingers to eat them. This includes olives, pickles, nuts, deviled eggs, and chips.

Sandwiches

The straightforward sandwich—that is, any sandwich that is not open-faced, not too tall to fit in the mouth, not saturated with dripping sauces or loaded with mushy fillings—is intended to be picked up and eaten. Otherwise use fork and knife.

Small fruits and berries on the stem

If you are served strawberries with the hulls on, cherries with stems, or grapes in bunches, then it is okay to eat them with your fingers. Otherwise, as with all berries, the utensil of choice is a spoon. In the case of grapes, you may encounter a special scissors, to be used to cut off a small cluster from the bunch. If not, tear a portion from the whole, rather than plucking off single grapes, which leaves a cluster of unattractive bare stems on the serving platter.

Bibliography

Anthony J. Strianese, *Dining and Banquet Management*, Second Edition, Delmer Publishers, 1997.

Christine Terhunne Herrick, ed. *Consolidated Library of Modern Cooking and Household Recipes*, New York: Bodmer, 1904

Edith A Wilkin, "Cleanliness Training Important", *Nation's Restaurant News*, 12 October 1987, 7

G. Jack Parisi, Director of Environmental Public Health Service, County of Schenectady, Schenectady, NY. Interview with author, 18 November 1995.

Janet McKenize Hill, *The Up-to-Date Waitress*, Boton: Little, Brown, and Co, 1906

John Love, *McDonald's behind the Arches*, Toronto: Bantam Books, 1986

Leon Gottlieb, *The Best of Gottlieb's Bottom Line*, New York: Lebhar Friedman, 1980.

Raymond J. Goodman, Jr., *The Management of Service for the Restaurant Manager*, 2nd Edition

INDEX